SYMBOLS & ABBREVIATIONS

The following symbols are used throughout this book:

ⓐ address　ⓣ telephone　ⓕ fax　ⓔ email　ⓦ website address
ⓛ opening times　ⓝ public transport connections　ⓘ important

The following symbols are used on the maps:

🄸 information office		○	city
✈ airport		○	large town
✚ hospital		○	small town
🛡 police station		═	motorway
🚌 bus station		─	main road
🚉 railway station		─	minor road
Ⓜ metro		─	railway
✝ cathedral			
❶ numbers denote featured cafés & restaurants			

Hotels and restaurants are graded by approximate price as follows:
£ budget　££ mid-range　£££ expensive

▶ *The cosmopolitan city*

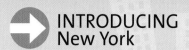

Introduction

New York has something for everyone, and the city is all about its people. From the very beginning, New York was destined to become great because of the vast variety of nationalities that immigrated to America, choosing to make it their home. People came from every nation, every race, and every walk of life. They embraced the freedom and opportunity they found in their new land, but they never shed their ethnic languages and customs. The people of New York hold tenaciously on to their traditions, and this is what gives the city its flavour. One-time mayor, John V Lindsay, had it right when he said, 'Not only is New York the nation's melting pot, it is also the casserole, the chafing dish, and the charcoal grill'.

Great leaders built New York with ambition and courage. Stock and bond trading, started more than 200 years ago by Alexander Hamilton, was the seedling of a world financial centre and a city so populous that its only way to grow was upwards – a literal forest of skyscrapers. Nestled in between are small neighbourhoods – enclaves such as Chinatown, Little Italy, or the Lower East Side with its Hebrew-signed storefronts. Urban grandeur is juxtaposed with small town charm – a place where a meatpacking stand becomes a hot fashion shop, or an avant-garde gallery.

New York is a forefront arts centre. Painters, musicians, and literary wordsmiths come to hone their skills in the city that never sleeps. Art collections span all interests, from a Tenement Museum to the palatial Metropolitan Museum of Art.

This is a city that sets a pace, from the Stock Exchange on Wall Street to soulful strains of a jazz trumpet. Its inhabitants are as comfortable in a suit and tie as they are in blue jeans; they'll munch on a pretzel from a street vendor alfresco in the morning, and dine on caviar at night with the same stride. They want to be seen, and at the same time they make the scene.

New Yorkers are inquisitive and enthusiastic, and they embrace the cultures around them; some 20,000 restaurants of every variety imaginable are testimony to this.

Could real estate, long ago acquired for a few beads and trinkets, be the downfall of this international metropolis, as towering glass invaders engulf once-charming neighbourhoods? Not likely. The people have a passion for their city despite its ever-changing complexion. As O'Henry wrote, 'It'll be a great place if they ever finish it!'

⬤ *The lights of New York's World Financial Center*

When to go

SEASONS & CLIMATE

Locals in New York say, 'If you don't like the weather, wait a minute.' The climate does have its swings, but is fairly predictable. Most surprising to visitors is how clear the air is in this dense city. April through to June is a favourable season, as people take to the streets and parks. Baseballs fly at Yankee Stadium, and cherry blossoms bloom in Brooklyn at the botanical garden. The spring freshness gives way to hot and humid weather in July and August, when families escape to the beaches. However, the city is then less crowded, and bargains can be found in shops and restaurants. The city wakes up from its summer siesta in September, and cultural venues start their programmes, horses pound the tracks at Belmont, and colourful autumn foliage sneaks into Central Park. Weather can be balmy right up to November, but when stormy northeast winds move in, expect snow or even a blizzard. New York can be crystal clear, yet brutally cold, when blistering winds blow through.

● *The Greek Independence Day parade on Fifth Avenue*

ANNUAL EVENTS

January
New Year's Eve The Times Square giant ball drops at the stroke of midnight, 200,000 people welcome in the New Year.
Ⓦ www.timessquarenyc.org

February
Chinese New Year Chinatown processions of lion dancers accompanied by clashing cymbals, gongs and drums on Mott Street.
Ⓦ www.chinatowninfo.com Ⓛ Festivities occur on several days

March
St Patrick's Day Parade Bagpipers and marching bands on Fifth Avenue, 44th to 86th Streets. ☏ 718 793 1600 Ⓛ 17 March

April
Cherry Blossom Festival Brooklyn Botanic Garden, including Japanese entertainment. Ⓦ www.bbg.org
Easter Parade Dates back to the 1800s. Spring strollers display imaginative, sometimes flamboyant, bonnets. ⓐ Fifth Avenue, 49th to 57th Streets ☏ 212 484 1222 Ⓛ Starts about 10.00

May
Animal Walk Ringling Bros and Barnum & Bailey Circus. An extraordinary parade of elephants and circus animals walks along 34th Street to Madison Square Garden at midnight!
Fleet Week Military ships parade up the Hudson River, and there is a formation fly-over of military aircraft. ⓐ Pier 86, W 46th Street & Twelfth Avenue ☏ 212 245 0072 Ⓦ www.intrepidmuseum.org
Ⓛ End May

Ninth Avenue International Food Festival A spread of food delicacies extending from 37th to 57th Streets on Ninth Avenue.

June

Celebrate Brooklyn Festival Multi-ethnic music, pop, jazz and rock at Prospect Park's Bandshell. ⓦ www.celebratebrooklyn.org

Museum Mile Festival Nine Museums offer free admission. ⓐ Fifth Avenue, 82nd Street ⓦ www.museummilefestival.org

July

Macy's 4th of July Fireworks Displays fly in the sky over the East River. Best seen on FDR Drive from East 14th to 41st Streets or Brooklyn Heights Promenade. ⓣ 212 494 4495

Midsummer Night Swing Big bands play jazz, Dixieland, R&B, calypso and Latin rhythms at an outdoor dance party at Lincoln Center's Fountain Plaza. ⓦ www.lincolncenter.org

August

Lincoln Center Out of Doors A month of music and dance. ⓦ www.lincolncenter.org

Howl! Festival Days of music and theatre, including **Wigstock**, a drag queen show. ⓐ Thompkins Square Park ⓦ www.howlfestival.com

September

Feast of San Gennaro Little Italy's feast honouring the patron saint of Naples. ⓐ Mulberry Street ⓦ www.sangennaro.org

Harlem Week Month-long Hispanic and black cultural event with food, gospel music and a film festival. ⓣ 212 862 7200

October
Greenwich Village Halloween Parade Delightful, humorous
31 October night-time parade; join in if you wear a costume.
🅐 Sixth Avenue from Spring Street to 23rd Street
🅦 www.halloween-nyc.com
New York Film Festival 🅐 Lincoln Center 🅦 www.filmlinc.com

November
New York City Marathon The 5-borough 42-km (26-mile) run starts
in Staten Island, and finishes in Central Park. 🅦 www.nyrr.org
Macy's Thanksgiving Day Parade Enormous helium-filled balloons
float over Central Park West. 🅐 77th Street down Broadway to Herald
Square 🅣 212 494 4495 🅛 Starts at 09.00, fourth Thur of Nov
Christmas Tree Lighting Ceremony The tree glitters with 25,000
bulbs at Rockefeller Center 🅣 212 332 6868

December
Christmas Windows Fifth Avenue stores display creative and
animated holiday windows. 🅦 www.nyctourist.com

PUBLIC HOLIDAYS

New Year's Day 1 January

Martin Luther King Day
   Third Mon in January

President's Day Third Mon
   in February

Easter Sunday

Independence Day 4 July

Labor Day First Mon in
   September

Columbus Day Second Mon
   in October

Memorial Day Last Mon in
   October

Veteran's Day 11 November

Thanksgiving Day Fourth
   Thur in November

Chanukah Eight days in
   December

Christmas Day 25 December

Central Park at its best

Summertime in New York is an all-out festival of culture. This is a time when locals and visitors escape the heat and humidity and go to the idyllic oasis of Central Park.

One hundred and fifty years ago, Frederick Law Olmstead converted swamp land into a pastoral park for New York's citizens who then lived in lower Manhattan. By the early 1900s, it contained many children's playgrounds, lakes, and a huge reservoir, sculptures, fountains, ball fields, a Carousel, the Wollman Rink, and several cafés. The park also had the Zoo and the elegant restaurant, Tavern on the Green. All of these continue today and, over the years, some 200 movies have been filmed in the park, such as *Barefoot in the Park* and *Godzilla*. The National Historic Landmark now stretches from 59th Street to 110th Street.

Free concerts and theatre took centre stage in the park during the 1960s, and these popular venues are still in place today. Surrounded by American Elms and a backdrop of skyscrapers, Central Park is New York's backyard, and from May through to Labor Day it is a sanctuary of the arts.

Shakespeare in the Park is sponsored by the Public Theater at the Delacorte Theater, and has star performers.

Metropolitan Opera and the **New York Philharmonic** take turns on The Great Lawn, the size of six ball fields. Thousands come to enjoy balmy evenings here, sometimes elbow to elbow, sitting on a blanket and eating a picnic in the open air.

Central Park SummerStage takes place at Rumsey Playfield with free weekday music – rock, blues, pop, ethnic, country and more.

One of the most romantic and popular ways to see Central Park is from a horse-drawn carriage. These operate year round and line up along Central Park South (59th Street) between Fifth and Sixth Avenues. ❶ 212 736 0680 Ⓦ www.centralparkcarriages.com

Alternatively, spend a night ice skating under the stars at Wollman Rink. ❶ 212 439 6900 Ⓛ Nov–end Mar

Stop a moment at Strawberry Fields to reflect on the memory of John Lennon and the Beatles' famous song.

For information see Ⓦ www.centralparknyc.org or read *New York's 50 Best Places to Discover* and *Enjoy in Central Park* by Karen Putnam and Marianne Cramer.

● *Take a blissful row through Central Park*

History

The first foreigner to arrive on the Hudson River, leading French explorers in 1554, was Giovanni da Verrazano. He was set on finding the Northwest Passage, a link between the Atlantic Ocean and Indian spice lands. Avoiding the river's strong currents, da Verrazano hightailed his way back out to sea.

Fifty-five years later, ignoring the route commissioned by the Dutch (to the Northeast from England along Greenland to Spitsbergen), it could be said that the British captain, Henry Hudson, discovered New York by accident when he sailed the *Half Moon* into the harbour of New York in September 1609. Enchanted with this lush land, he continued all the way up the river to Albany.

The area around the Hudson River was inhabited by Algonquin Lenape Native Americans, who had been in the area for thousands of years. The importance of Hudson's expedition became apparent in 1624 when Governor's Island was settled as a Dutch trading post, with Flemish Walloon families. Two years later Dutch-born Peter Minuit acquired Manhattan Island (a Lenape name) for the legendary sum of $24 worth of beads.

From the beginning, Manhattan, a part of New Amsterdam, was a melting pot of diverse nationalities, seafarers and smugglers. When things became unruly, Peg-Leg-Pete, also known as Peter Stuyvesant, stepped in. His strict style and intolerance was admonished by his Dutch superiors.

James, Duke of York, brother to King Charles II, asserted the British claim to the area. In 1664, British warships arrived and took New York (named after the Duke), without a shot fired.

Lutherans, Jews, Catholics, Quakers, and Dutch Reformists were resident on the island. African slaves came in ships, against their will, making up 15–20 per cent of the population. They built much of the city, its roads, and worked on farms, and in the busy port.

Conflict between the British and their American colonies was growing, hastened by heavy taxation. In 1775, battles broke out in Massachusetts, starting the American Revolution.

Facing 100 British warships in the harbour, with an impressive army of 30,000 troops, George Washington had the Declaration of Independence read to his assembled troops. Washington waged war to defend New York, but, after heavy losses, retreated. After seven years, the tides turned and Washington marched into Manhattan to claim victory. From 1783 to 1790, New York was capital of the United States of America. On 30 April 1789, Washington was inaugurated as first president of the country at Federal Hall on Wall Street.

Years of prosperity followed. New York became a leading financial and shipping centre. Its burgeoning population still lived below Houston Street – a hemlock forest covered most of the city. New Yorkers started their trek northward. By the early 1830s, wealthy citizens were living as far north as Greenwich Village. When Central Park was made, and with the advent of train travel, locals continued to move northward, all the way to Harlem.

New York's other boroughs were connected by bridges and tunnels, including the adored Brooklyn Bridge and, by 1898, the outer boroughs (Brooklyn, Queens, Staten Island and the Bronx) officially became a part of the city.

Over the next century, New York's population grew to a staggering 8 million, and today is one of the most influential cities in the world.

Lifestyle

Where are all those people going? As you watch an energetic crowd crossing the avenues of midtown Manhattan, this is the question that comes to mind.

On weekdays, when workers and visitors fill up the city, Manhattan's population increases sevenfold from its resident base of 1.5 million – that's a mass of 11 million on the move!

City slickers work hard, but New York is an adult playground: inhabitants appreciate the wide-ranging eateries, cafés, boutiques, nightlife, and neighbourhoods.

Move over *Breakfast at Tiffany's*, here comes the real *Sex and the City*. New Yorkers want to look fabulous walking on the street, and show off their shopping spree, perhaps a pair of shoes from **Jimmy Choos**. They love to hang out, too. Check out the after-work scene at any bar, such as **O'Neal's Grand Bar**, a once-upon-a-time speakeasy.

New Yorkers love to relax, too. Hence the opening of **BED New York**, also on *Sex and the City*'s list, where customers shed their shoes, fall into pillows, and nibble on bed bites while sipping a vodka-based drink called 'Heavy Petting'.

New York is what you want it to be. Anyone can find a comfort zone in the city, whatever their predisposition. New York is at once the most American of cities and the least American of cities – it is a *world* city.

▶ *Enter, eat, relax at BED New York*

Culture

Despite its relatively short life in the timeline of art history, New York houses an almost unrivalled collection of art in its museums and galleries. Philanthropic movers and shakers of New York's early years helped to establish the city as an arts capital.

The same man who founded New York's first savings bank, John Pintard, helped to organise The New York Historical Society, which became the city's first museum in 1804.

In 1870, the Metropolitan Museum of Art was founded and showed works of Hals and Van Dyck, along with other famous European artists. Today, it is one of the largest museums in the world, with vast collections that could take weeks to see.

The desire to collect has been in the heart of Americans for most of the country's young history, and it continues today. Prosperity from the fur trade, oil, coal, steel, gold, shipping, the railway, and even from horse breeding, found its way to the arts.

During the 19th and 20th centuries, merchants, industrialists, financiers, and heirs to America's fortunes contributed to and founded museums, universities and libraries. Among them are names that punctuate the New York landscape, in particular, Museum Mile on Fifth Avenue – Solomon Guggenheim, John Jacob Astor, Henry Clay Frick, Andrew Carnegie, William Henry Vanderbilt and Gertrude Vanderbilt Whitney.

Modern works were first exhibited at the 'Armory Show of 1913', showing European paintings by Cezanne, Gauguin, Van Gogh, Picasso and Kandinsky. 'Abstract expressionism' brought New York under the world's spotlight, with names like Jackson Pollock, Willem

▶ *The Metropolitan Museum of Art is a temple for historians*

de Kooning, and Mark Rothko. Later came Andy Warhol and the pop era. New York has museums and galleries tucked into corners of every borough and neighbourhood. Many are found in Chelsea, SoHo, Brooklyn, and on Madison Avenue.

Programmes sell out early at the amazing Lincoln Center – a prime venue for jazz, opera, ballet and theatre. Try for a stand-by ticket at the box office.

Then there is Broadway, the 'Great White Way', with 40 theatres around Times Square. Experimental and less expensive are Off-Broadway and Off-Off-Broadway theatres, mostly located in the Village and SoHo. Off-Broadway theatres on Hudson and Bleecker Streets offer productions of interest to gay and lesbian audiences. Many hotels can assist in obtaining show tickets.

Tickets for same-day performances, often with healthy discounts (expect queues), can be found at TKTS Booth (ⓐ 47th Street at Broadway ⓣ 212 221 0013 ⓦ www.tdf.org), or purchase full price through Ticketmaster (ⓣ 212 307 4100 ⓦ www.ticketmaster.com), Showlistings (ⓦ www.playbill.com or ⓦ www.theatermania.com)

Summertime brings many free alfresco cultural events to Central Park, Bryant Park, and Brooklyn's Prospect Park, among others. Tom Wolfe wrote of New York that 'Culture just seems to be in the air, like part of the weather'.

September's annual 17-day **New York Film Festival** (ⓣ Box Office 212 875 5050 ⓦ www.filmlinc.com) showcases emerging talent at Lincoln Center. **NewFest** (ⓣ 212 254 7228 ⓦ www.newfest.org), the New York Lesbian & Gay Film Festival, runs for about ten days in early June. The free and eclectic rag, the *Village Voice*, has comprehensive listings of what's going on around the city.

▶ *New York is a city that never sleeps*

Shopping

The shopping scene in New York is nothing less than seductive. You can buy anything, and shop until your pockets are running on empty. Macy's is the world's largest must-see store, and there are the other shopping institutions, Bloomingdale's, and Sak's.

Window shop on Fifth Avenue from 49th to 59th Street; take in the pricey delights of Tiffany & Co; revisit your childhood at FAO Schwartz toy store; meet up with Mickey Mouse at the Disney Store; enjoy a tumbling waterfall at Trump Tower; get over a bad date at Armani or Bulgari; or pack up at Louis Vuitton.

'I CAN GET IT FOR YOU WHOLESALE'

This is a New York expression as old as the city (remember those beads?)

No need to break the bank – try some of these treasures:

Aaron's Brooklyn's answer to discount designer.
Ⓦ www.aarons.com

Century 21 Family clothing, 25–75 per cent off.
Ⓦ www.c21stores.com

INA Designer men's and women's consignment handbags, jeans, dresses. Ⓐ Uptown, downtown, and Chinatown
Ⓦ www.inanyc.com

Jack's 99 Cent Store Ⓐ 110 W 32nd Street

Orchard Street The inventor of 'discount'. Ⓛ Closed Sat, jammed on Sun

SSS Sample Sale Garment centre overstock.
Ⓦ www.clothingline.com

Strand Bookstore Eighteen miles of books.
Ⓦ www.strandbooks.com

You can slip over to the MoMA (Museum of Modern Art) on W 54th Street for cutting edge gift designs, and the museums have some of the more eclectic items to buy in the city.

Nick-named 'Gold Coast', but looking more like a Paris fashion catwalk, Madison Avenue above 50th Street is home to very expensive designer boutiques. Start at Barney's, cruise by Valentino, Dolce & Gabbana, Givenchy and Carolina Herrera, see shimmering crystal at Baccarat, or visit the chef-at-home paradise, Williams-Sonoma.

Hot fashion trends and crafts are found off the main drag in the Meatpacking District (Stella McCartney and Diane von Furstenberg), and even in Harlem (Sistahs of Harlem street couture at Pieces boutique). Don't miss Bleecker Street or the less pricey Lower East Side.

Open-air markets have delicious food at Union Square, and the Malcom Shabazz Harlem Market sells textiles. Buy California wines at Astor Place, and sourdough at numerous bakeries. Don't try to haggle.

Normal opening hours are 09.00 or 10.00 to 18.00, Monday to Saturday, but nothing is normal in New York City and many shops stay open until 21.00 as well as opening on Sundays.

● *Macy's is every shopper's paradise*

Eating & drinking

There must be a restaurant in New York for each of the world's dialects. New York is graced with 20,000 eating establishments, not counting street vendors, bars and cafés.

SHORT HISTORY

Opened in 1827, Delmonico's was the first restaurant in the US. For two decades in the mid 1800s, Charles Renhofer, considered to be America's greatest chef of the time, invented trademark dishes for the restaurant that are still popular today: Lobster Newburg, Baked Alaska, Steak Delmonico and Eggs Benedict.

● *Elegant art deco style at Petrossian Restaurant*

AMERICAN FARE

As the saying goes, there is nothing more American than apple pie, except, perhaps, French fries! Not to be missed is a big juicy steak, cooked rare, of course. On Thanksgiving Day, a strictly American holiday, dine on food native to North America – turkey with cranberry sauce on the side, sweet potatoes, corn on the cob, mashed yams, and pumpkin pie.

Bounty from the sea brings tender lobsters (not at all like langoustine sold in Europe), oysters, steamers, and Manhattan clam chowder to the American menu.

Fast foods include doughnuts and hot dogs (the latter from Germany). The earliest example of a hot dog dates back to the 1860s. The poor mistreated hamburger has a very mixed history, but, suffice to say, the really good ones are found in delis and diners, or in an American home.

Popular foods considered American but with foreign origins include the blintz and knish from Eastern Europe; bagels, and salmon lox brought in by Jews; soul food from Africa; and Southwestern or tacos from Mexico.

Despite the disappearance of famous old markets (the meatpackers on 14th Street and fish stands at Fulton), fresh produce of high quality, and an extensive variety of foods are easily found in the city.

COUNTING PENNIES

Restaurants with prestigious reputations can be ruthlessly expensive. A new concept has evolved, and famous chefs are reaching out to a broader public with informal restaurants in emerging neighbourhoods. The new eateries emphasise quality menus, and some of them are amazingly reasonable. New Yorkers order an entrée and salad, often skipping appetisers, desserts and coffee unless they're out for a romantic evening. Portions tend to be large, and include a complement of vegetables. An entrée-only meal means you can eat haute cuisine and not break the bank. Smoking is illegal in restaurants.

Regional growers bring fresh produce to open-air markets daily. The largest, at Union Square, is open Mon, Wed, Fri and Sat 08.00–18.00. It's a great place to meet locals and to forage for picnic ingredients (fresh baked breads, local honey and just-ripe fruits). Picnic in Washington Square Park, or go west on 14th Street to a small triangular park near the Hudson River for a leisurely lunch.

LIQUID TREATS

Look for California wines on the menu: Napa Valley's aromatic Cabernet Sauvignon, or Pinot Noir and Chardonnay from Sonoma. Try Robert Mondavi's Stag's Leap, or Kendall Jackson.

Bars and Lounges are abundant and hot. Some stay open until dawn, and offer libations with enticing names. Not into alcohol? Try a smoothie – a healthy version of the milkshake with blended mixed fruits and juice – or a speciality coffee at one of many cafés.

PRACTICAL DETAILS

A good time to visit is during Restaurant Week, a bi-annual event held in July. Fine restaurants and notable chefs (Jean-Georges, David Burke) offer *prix fixe* menus: lunch $24.07 (pun intended), that's about £13; dinner $35, which is about £19.

RESTAURANT CATEGORIES
Average price of main dish without drinks:
£ up to $24; ££ $25–$46; £££ above $46

Reserve ahead online (W www.opentable.com), or perhaps call last minute to pick up a cancellation. Alternatively, reserve a table for an early hour. Locals usually eat between 19.00 and 21.00, but kitchens stay open much later, some into the night. The most popular restaurants are sometimes reserved months in advance.

When it's time to pay, ask for the 'bill'. Credit cards are accepted in most restaurants. To lighten the burden, check online for discount coupons (W www.restaurant.com). Tax is extra, plus customary gratuities – 15–20 per cent – double the tax to work out the tip. Tipping is usually up to the customer, but for larger parties tips can be mandatory, as stated on the menu.

Try a different cuisine at every meal. Does Thai, Turkish or Ethiopian sound enticing? Work off the calories later!

● Grab a hot dog to keep you going

Entertainment & nightlife

People come to New York with a burning desire to, as the song 'New York, New York' says, 'become king of the hill, top of the heap'.

Simply put, New York is at the cutting edge and global crossroads of entertainment – from house to hip-hop or from Samba to Salsa – and beyond. Music is everywhere. It bursts from passing boom boxes on sidewalks; soulful trumpets blaze underground on a subway platform; and techno rips all night long at the clubs.

The 1920s Harlem Renaissance filled Big Apple clubs with jazz and blues, and performers like Louis Sachmo Armstrong or Count Basie. Visitors can reminisce about the era today at the Apollo Theater. The venue that launched music greats, such as Ella Fitzgerald and Michael Jackson, still showcases new talent.

Making people laugh is the goal of improvisational comedians at Chelsea's wacky, Upright Citizens Brigade Theater, and in Times Square. Broadway theatre is booming, ever since the sleaze around Times Square was cleaned up during the 1990s. There's a renaissance of Tin Pan Alley pop and Broadway musicals in small café society cabaret venues all around the city.

Nothing could ever match that icon of icons, Studio 54, but cavernous disco clubs are pretty much gone. High calibre night-owl DJs spin records to the wee hours, dishing out IDM, straight-up techno, microhouse, hip-hop, drum 'n' bass, or punk in clubs that come and go like waves. Many are in trendy neighbourhoods like Chelsea, the Meatpacking District and SoHo. Getting past the velvet rope may require a charm school degree; go on weekdays when hip New Yorkers go out, and expect to pay the bill with cash.

Check the web at ⓦ www.partythisweek.com for up-to-date information and listings for nightclubs, lounges, and parties.

❶ Have ID to hand – not your passport – even if you're over 40; be nice to the doorman; what you wear really matters; spend weekend nights anywhere else as the clubs will be very crowded; prepare for a pricey night, and, oh yes, bring cash, and take a cab to get home.

⬤ Times Square – a place that never sleeps

Sport & relaxation

Escaping hustle and bustle is a prime occupation of New Yorkers. They actively participate in sports, and avidly support their home teams as spectators. Contrary to preconceptions, the city is not all bricks and mortar; it's the greenest city in the US – more than a quarter of New York is devoted to parks and open space.

Central Park is Manhattan's backyard. Joggers and runners pace off around the soft surface reservoir track – 2.5 km (1.6 miles). Bicyclers circle the entire park on three park drives; the longest is 10 km (6.1 miles). Bicycle and rowing boat rentals are available at Loeb Boathouse (❶ 212 517 2233 ● Mar–end Oct).

Other activities in the park include: inline skates or roller skates rentals for $15/£8 (❶ 212 396 1010); wall climbing at North Meadow $7/£4 (❶ 212 348 4867x10); horseback riding on the park bridle paths – horse rental from nearby Claremont Stables (❶ 212 724 5100).

It's not the Matterhorn, but come the first snowfall, locals brush the dust off their skis and go cross-country skiing in Sheep Meadow or on the Great Lawn. At spring's first bloom there is bird-watching, weekend Yoga, and *yang*-style Tai Chi lessons at the North Meadow Recreation Center for a moderate fee (● www.centralparknyc.org ● The park is closed from 01.00–06.00).

Those who prefer to run along a river waterfront use the Hudson River Park jogging path that extends all the way from Battery Park to the George Washington Bridge. Spend a day sailing with Come Sail New York! (● Liberty Landing, Jersey City, NJ ❶ 201 887 8700 ● www.sailthehudson.com) Give a boost to the abs at the Chelsea Piers – health spa, golf driving range, rollerblade rink on the roof – all with a spectacular view.

New Yorkers worship their home teams, starting with the national pastime sport – baseball. The Yankees play at Yankee Stadium in the Bronx, and the Mets at Shea Stadium in Queens.

Madison Square Garden hosts the adored Knicks basketball team, as well as ice hockey's Rangers. Football games are at Giants Stadium in Meadowlands' sports complex, across the Hudson River in New Jersey. Tickets for most sporting events can be purchased through Ticketmaster (Ⓦ www.ticketmaster.com). The US Tennis Open (Ⓦ www.tickco.com) and Aqueduct Race Track are in Queens.

● Get your skates on at the Rockefeller outdoor ice-rink

Accommodation

There are so many hotels in New York that choosing one can be daunting. Millions of people move about every day, and there are not enough rooms to cover all the tourists, and people in town for meetings and conventions. If you arrive during Fashion Week or when the president visits, the city can be at a complete standstill. At such times, hotel rooms can be impossible to find, especially the more economical ones. The solution is to book early or to book in January or July (but you'll have to reckon with the weather). Be sure to look for special deals such as on weekends. Many hotels are economical enough that visitors can stay right in the city. It's possible to lay your head down for a dreamy sleep in a bunk bed (dreamy, because you're paying $50/£27 or less for the night). Yet if splurge is your goal, find a hotel that offers iPod docking stations, Bulgari bath amenities, bathroom scales that measure pounds *and* kilos, and the ubiquitous shoeshine.

There are plenty of chain hotels around the city with reasonable rates. The hotels listed here are a combination of economic hostels, budget hotels with charm (but that may have shared bathrooms), and hotels that are old world favourites. As neighbourhoods gentrified, hotels popped on to the scene. There is quite a bit of choice in a variety of neighbourhoods.

PRICE RATINGS
The following price guides are based on the cost of a room for two people per night. Room tax and breakfast are not included in price unless indicated.
£ Up to $175; ££ $175 to $300; £££ Over $300

Americana Inn £ Great Times Square location, small hotel with mini-sink in each room, shared bathroom and kitchenette. 69 W 38th Street 212 840 6700 212 840 1830 www.newyorkhotel.com

Chelsea International Hostel £ In historic Chelsea, this hostel provides sheets, and has an internet café. 251 W 20th Street 212 647 0010 212 727 7289 www.chelseahostel.com

Gershwin Hotel £ This Tin Pan Alley Greek Revival hotel/hostel has its accent on pop art, and lots of fun. 7 E 27th Street 212 545 8000 212 684 5546 www.gershwinhotel.com

Hostelling International New York £ On the Upper West Side, this large hostel organises good walking tours. 891 Amsterdam Avenue 212 932 2300 212 932 2574 www.hinewyork.org

Larchmont Hotel £ A small beaux arts townhouse fits right into the Village, shared bathroom, continental breakfast. 27 W 11th Street 212 989 9333 212 989 9496 www.larchmonthotel.com

Hotel Pennsylvania £ This huge hotel has seen glory in Duke Ellington days, now it's economical and well located. 401 Seventh Avenue 212 736 5000 212 502 8712 www.hotelpenn.com

The SoHoTel £ Good value in NoLita (North of Little Italy), small rooms, most with private bathroom; an upgrade gets vaulted ceilings. 341 Broome Street 212 226 1482 212 226 3525 www.sohotel-ny.com

Vanderbilt YMCA £ Steps from the United Nations, the 'Y' is well located for tourist sites – single and double rooms with TV. 🅐 224 E 47th Street (also located in Harlem, West Side, Brooklyn) 🅣 212 756 9600 🅕 212 752 0210 🅦 www.ymcanyc.org

Hotel Belleclaire £–££ A landmark hotel near Lincoln Center, it has goose-down comforters, some rooms have shared bathrooms. 🅐 250 W 77th Street 🅣 212 362 7700 🅕 212 362 1004 🅦 www.hotelbelleclaire.com

Washington Square Hotel £–££ Once a haven for artists, the hotel has a comfy bar, pleasant rooms, a complimentary breakfast and afternoon tea. 🅐 103 Waverly Place 🅣 212 777 9515 🅕 212 979 8373 🅦 www.washingtonsquarehotel.com

Abingdon Guest House ££ European flavour and four-poster beds are a treat in this tiny, artistically decorated Meatpacking District house. 🅐 13 Eighth Avenue 🅣 212 243 5384 🅕 212 807 7473 🅦 www.abingdonguesthouse.com

Hotel Edison ££ This large Art deco hotel has giant wall murals in the lobby, and is next to Times Square. 🅐 228 W 47th Street 🅣 212 840 5000 🅕 212 596 6850 🅦 www.edisonhotel.com

Hudson Hotel ££ Renovated with daring colours, this hotel with tiny rooms boasts trendy people, and a roof terrace. 🅐 356 W 58th Street 🅣 212 554 6000 🅕 212 554 6001 🅦 www.hudsonhotel.com

◀ *The Gershwin Hotel is truly a unique place to stay*

On the Avenue ££ Close to Lincoln Center, with charming, stylish rooms, there's a viewing balcony only for guests. ⓐ 2178 Broadway ⓘ 212 362 1100 ⓕ 787 9521 ⓦ www.ontheave-nyc.com

Hotel QT ££ At this stylish hotel, swim in the lobby pool, or get free wi-fi internet access and flat-screen TV shows in each room. ⓐ 125 W 45th Street ⓘ 212 354 2323 ⓕ 212 328 585 ⓦ www.hotelqt.com

Hotel Thirty Thirty ££ Situated on a quiet street in the Murray Hill area, this renovated hotel is quite affordable. ⓐ 30 E 30th Street ⓘ 212 689 1900 ⓕ 212 689 0023 ⓦ www.thirtythirty-nyc.com

Wall Street District Hotel ££ In the financial epicentre, this hotel has high-tech amenities for its guests. ⓐ 15 Gold Street ⓘ 212 232 7700 ⓕ 212 232 7746 ⓦ www.wallstreetdistricthotel.com

Gansevoort £££ This towering hotel has full-service luxury in the Meatpacking District. Relax at the roof garden pool. ⓐ 18 Ninth Avenue ⓘ 212 206 6700 ⓕ 212 255 5858 ⓦ www.hotelgansevoort.com

Library Hotel £££ This luxury boutique hotel has a poetry garden; read a book while having afternoon tea. ⓐ 299 Madison Avenue ⓘ 212 983 4500 ⓕ 212 499 9099 ⓦ www.libraryhotel.com

The Lowell £££ An ultra-luxury boutique hotel on the Upper East Side that has suites with working fireplaces, Bulgari amenities and a regal afternoon tea in the Pembroke Room. ⓐ 28 E 63rd Street ⓘ 212 838 1400 ⓕ 212 319 4230 ⓦ www.lowellhotel.com

Pierre £££ This landmark, old-world luxury hotel is the limelight of the Grand Army Plaza on Central Park. ⓐ 2 E 61st Street ⓣ 212 838 8000 ⓕ 212 940 8109 ⓦ www.tajhotels.com/pierre

60 Thompson £££ A designer hotel in SoHo with a chic mood, a guest-only rooftop, modern rooms and down duvets. ⓐ 60 Thompson Street ⓣ 212 431 0400 ⓕ 212 431 0200 ⓦ www.60thompson.com

Waldorf-Astoria £££ This hotel put Waldorf Salad on the planet, and you can't get any better than this huge historic landmark. ⓐ 301 Park Avenue ⓣ 212 355 3000 ⓕ 212 872 7272 ⓦ www.waldorf.com

⬤ *The Waldorf is a New York icon*

THE BEST OF NEW YORK

Some people visit New York in a mad dash, but, if you're wise, you'll linger longer in this wonderful city. There is so much on offer, it's hard to choose what to do, but here are some places that should not be missed.

TOP 10 ATTRACTIONS

- **Eclectic Neighbourhoods** Hot, trendy areas to stroll (see pages 118–131)

- **Empire State Building** Spectacular 360-degree city views (see page 60).

- **Great White Way** Theatre-goers' hunting ground (see page 63).

- **Lincoln Center** Performing arts bliss (see pages 100–101).

- **Museum Mile** Nine great museums in a row (see page 44).

- **Radio City Music Hall** Rockettes kick eye-high (see page 73).

- **Rockefeller Center** A multi-building world of art deco (see pages 63–4).

- **Statue of Liberty/Ellis Island** See how visitors are greeted. 'Huddled masses yearning to breathe free' (see page 79).

- **United Nations** The world meets here (see page 65).

- **Wall Street** Where it all began (see pages 79–80).

The unmistakable vista of New York at night

Here are some time-conscious guides to visiting the city, whether you're between business appointments, or when you're settling in:

HALF-DAY: NEW YORK IN A HURRY

Start off in Times Square and have a look around Broadway. From there, go eastwards on 59th Street, passing by Radio City Music Hall. Stroll down the Channel Gardens at Rockefeller Plaza to where the statue of Prometheus gazes over the ice-skating rink. Catch your breath, then walk northwards on Fifth Avenue. Pop into St Patrick's Cathedral, and window shop all the way to 59th Street and Central Park.

If there's time, hop on a subway down to the end of town. The Statue of Liberty is visible from Battery Park. On the way back uptown, enjoy a bird's-eye-view of Manhattan and far beyond from the Empire State Building's lofty observation platform. Are you feeling really flush? You can do all this and more in a mere 15 minutes – on a helicopter ride that gives views of all five boroughs (ⓦ www.libertyhelicopters.com).

1 DAY: TIME TO SEE A LITTLE MORE

Consider the above half-day itinerary, but start on the free, half-hour Staten Island Ferry for a closer look at Ellis Island and famous Lady Liberty. Alternatively, take the Circle Line for a two-hour cruise that skirts around half of Manhattan. Spend some time in the museum of your choice, perhaps the Museum of Modern Art on your way up Fifth Avenue. Eat a hot dog on the run before exploring the twisty streets of Greenwich Village or some of New York's eclectic neighbourhoods in SoHo, Chelsea or the Lower East Side. In the evening, dine with locals, or listen to some jazz.

2–3 DAYS: SHORT CITY-BREAK

Buy a City Pass (ⓦ www.citypass.com), which covers entry to several sights, and hop-on, hop-off Gray Line's loop tours that run the length of Manhattan from Wall Street to Harlem, plus some important sections of Brooklyn. Explore ethnic neighbourhoods in Chinatown and Queens. Take your time at a zoo, or botanical garden, and have a picnic break.

Visit the United Nations, or the Cathedral of St John the Divine. Explore Grand Central Terminal and savour fruits of the sea at the Oyster Bar. Marvel at the medieval collection at the Cloisters. Wonder at the indoor Ferris Wheel at Toys R Us in Times Square before seeing a theatre performance, then stay up all night dancing to a techno beat.

> *'As only New Yorkers know, if you can get through the twilight, you'll live through the night.'*
> Dorothy Parker.

LONGER: ENJOYING NEW YORK CITY TO THE FULL

Spend some days seeing the treasures housed along Museum Mile, especially at the Metropolitan Museum of Art. Go further afield to explore more city treasures in Brooklyn, Queens and the Bronx.

Something for nothing

It's easy to spend a week or more enjoying New York and spending very little. Popular pastimes are street fairs, open-air markets and festivals. You can find a flea market nearly any day of the week, a good source is www.keysfleamarket.com. Hell's Kitchen and Smith Street Brooklyn flea markets are both open on weekends (ⓦ www.hellskitchenfleamarket.com).

Check local newspapers, or do a little online planning at ⓦ www.nycvisit.com before arrival. Keep an ear tuned in for the sound of music; you might hear outdoor lunchtime concerts or street musicians from spring through to autumn.

Local volunteers from Big Apple Greeters introduce you to the city, or to their own neighbourhood, for free (ⓣ 212 669 8159

🔺 New York is bustling 24–7

Ⓦ www.bigapplegreeter.org). Who says New Yorkers aren't friendly? Some neighbourhoods have free walking tours. Summer tours of 8th Street and the Greenwich Village Historic area start at St Mark's Place (Ⓦ www.villagealliance.org).

Big Onion Tours (Ⓦ www.bigonion.com) explores the Wall Street area and Harlem. The free Downtown Connection bus travels from Chambers Street around Manhattan's tip to South Street Seaport, making a dozen stops (Ⓦ www.downtownny.com). For fresh air, take the Staten Island Ferry, better still, kayak on the Hudson River for free from the Downtown Boathouse (Ⓦ www.downtownboathouse.org).

Visit the National Museum of the American Indian, which is devoted to the history and art of Native Americans. Many small, interesting museums charge no fee, such as Forbes Galleries with toy soldiers and presidential manuscripts (Ⓦ www.forbesgalleries.com), or the Museum at FIT (Fashion Institute of Technology) devoted to fashion (Ⓦ www.fitnyc.edu/museum). Summertime brings free alfresco film screenings to Bryant Park.

Learn about the birds and bees at Queens Botanical Garden (Ⓦ www.queensbotanical.org). Brooklyn Botanic Garden (Ⓦ www.bbg.org) has no fee all day on Tuesdays. The Bronx Zoo is free on Wednesdays (Ⓦ www.bronxzoo.com). Try catch-and-release fishing for bass or sunfish at The Meer in Central Park where bamboo fishing poles are provided free.

New York's diverse architecture will lead you into gothic churches and art deco skyscrapers.

Be part of a television show audience or head underground at Times Square subway station, where live music is in the air. If blues is your thing, top off the night at B B King's club for free, live music (Ⓦ www.bbkingblues.com).

When it rains

New Yorkers go about their business come rain or shine. Perhaps they've adopted the post-office motto that is inscribed on its landmark beaux arts building: 'Neither snow nor rain nor heat nor gloom of night stays these couriers from the swift completion of their appointed rounds.'

If the weather is cold or wet, spend some time shopping in Macy's, the block-long department store, or in the store of your choice. Gaze at the stars on the Sky Ceiling at Grand Central Station on a twice-weekly free tour.

Explore the Museum of Modern Art and take home some unique gifts from the shop – where else can you get an 'I love Spanish Harlem' T-shirt?

MUSEUM MILE

There are nine museums, one after another, along this famous Fifth Avenue mile, running downtown from 104th Street. If you start at the Metropolitan Museum of Art, you'll probably end up there for the whole day. Museums all have cafés. Museums here are listed as the traffic flows:

El Museo del Barrio-Latino Art, paintings, sculpture, pre-Columbian.

Neue Galerie Museum for German and Austrian Art Art and design, Café Sabarsky (see page 92).

Jewish Museum Jewish culture and art, kosher Café Weissman.

The National Academy of Design Two centuries of American art.

Goethe-Institut New York Features German artists, concerts, film.

If you don't want to work out at the gym, you can luxuriate at Elizabeth Arden's Red Door. You can catch up on your email at the New York Public Library, another splendid beaux arts building, and you can take one of their free tours (Ⓦ www.nypl.org).

If you take the Gray Line tour, don't worry, they courteously provide rain ponchos.

So it's raining, so what? If rain falls while you're on the subway, be sure that an enterprising entrepreneur will be at the exit selling umbrellas, cheap. Central Park offers free guided walking tours and themed tours, rain or shine, year round – but not in blizzards (Ⓦ www.centralparknyc.org/activities/walkingtours).

🔺 *Who can resist a trip to Macy's?*

On arrival

TIME DIFFERENCES

New York follows Eastern Standard Time (EST). During Daylight Saving Time (mid Mar to early Nov), clocks are put ahead one hour, and during these months, at 12.00 noon in New York, time elsewhere is as follows:

Australia Eastern Standard Time 02.00, Central Standard Time 01.30, Western Standard Time 24.00
New Zealand 04.00
South Africa 18.00
UK and Republic of Ireland 17.00
USA and Canada Newfoundland Time 13.30, Atlantic Canada Time 13.00, Eastern Time noon, Central Time 11.00, Mountain Time 10.00, Pacific Time 09.00, Alaska 08.00

ARRIVING

Arriving by air

Two major international airports serve New York, and
ⓦ www.panynj.gov gives detailed airport and transportation information on all New York airports. The largest, **John F. Kennedy Airport**, known as JFK (ⓣ 718 244 4444) is 24 km (15 miles) from Midtown Manhattan. Each of its nine terminals has currency exchange, ATM and car rental. For public transit, follow signs marked 'Ground Transportation' to exit the airport.
Taxis (ⓣ 212 692 8294 ⓦ www.nyc.gov/taxi) – 'yellow cabs' – wait outside the baggage claim, taking 30–60 minutes to Manhattan, $45/£24 flat fee plus tolls and 15 per cent tip. ⓘ Accept rides only from uniformed agents at the taxi stand. Shared vans cost half the

price, with door-to-door service, but they make several stops; one is SuperShuttle (☎ 212 209 7000 Ⓦ www.supershuttle.com).

Buses from New York Airport Service (☎ 718 875 8200 Ⓦ www.nyairportservice.com) take the same amount of time as taxis, departing every 15–30 minutes for about $12/£6 to Grand Central Terminal, Penn Station, and Port Authority Bus Station; it costs about $8/£4 more for a hotel shuttle service from Grand Central to hotels between 33rd and 57th Streets.

Subway (an underground metro) alternatives that avoid congested traffic are far cheaper than going by road, but are tedious, cumbersome and time-consuming. AirTrain (☎ 800 626 7433) costs $5/£3 and connects to the subway for an additional $2/£1. ❶ AirTrain is free for connections between JFK's terminals, parking areas and rental car facilities.

Newark Liberty Airport (☎ 973 961 6000) is located in New Jersey, 26 km (16 miles) away from the city, and also services the New York metro area. Taxis to the centre cost about $40–$60/£21–£32. Buses cost $13–$19/£7–£10, and depart from the 'Ground Transportation' area. **Newark Liberty Airport Express** connects to the Port Authority Bus Terminal and the train stations, as well as to Chinatown and the Wall Street area. **AirTrain** costs about $11/£6 and connects to Penn Station via the new Rail Link Station. Follow signs marked 'Monorail/AirTrain Link'.

Fiorello LaGuardia Airport (☎ 718 533 3400) services mostly domestic flights, plus Canada and the Caribbean, and it is only 14 km (9 miles) from Manhattan. Metered taxi rides run from $16–$26/ £9–£14 for the 20-minute ride to midtown. Buses and shared van services are similar in cost to JFK.

Whichever airport you use, remember that traffic can be treacherous; leave early for flights, and avoid illegal 'gypsy' cabs.

Arriving by rail

Pennsylvania Station (🚇 33rd Street, between 7th and 8th Avenues 📞 800 872 7245) on New York's West Side is home to **Amtrak** trains (📞 800 872 7245 🌐 www.amtrak.com) arriving from all over the US. It also serves Long Island and New Jersey. **Grand Central Terminal** (🚇 42nd Street at Park Avenue 📞 212 532 4900 🌐 www.grandcentralterminal.com) is across town on the East Side, and

🔺 *Landmarks such as the Empire State Building help you get your bearings*

primarily serves commuter destinations in the suburbs. Both stations have a full complement of tourist amenities, some noted restaurants, and are easily reached by taxi, bus or subway.

Arriving by bus

Port Authority Bus Terminal at Eighth Avenue between 40th and 42nd Streets is a busy place, but organised (☎ 212 564 8484), with connections to nearly everywhere on the North American continent. Amenities are vast, and include a post office, ATM, parking, and even a bowling alley.

Driving in New York

Manhattan is mostly laid out on a grid pattern, but some areas are a confusing jumble of streets. It's *right-hand* drive in the US, and parking rates in New York run up to $40/£21 a day. Each weekday morning, most bridges and tunnels are closed to single inbound drivers for four hours.

Simply put, *don't* drive; do what New Yorkers do and use public transportation. The subway runs underground and avoids the snarled traffic just above.

If driving is a must, reserve parking through **Icon Parking Systems** (🌐 www.weparknewyork.com). Car rental can be arranged at the airport, and national rental companies such as **Avis** (☎ 212 421 5319 🌐 www.avis.com) have several many locations in the city. Rates tend to be high in the New York area.

FINDING YOUR FEET

From every approach to the city, travellers get a glimpse of the great skyscrapers high above Manhattan island's granite base. You should get your bearings by taking a brief walk around your hotel's

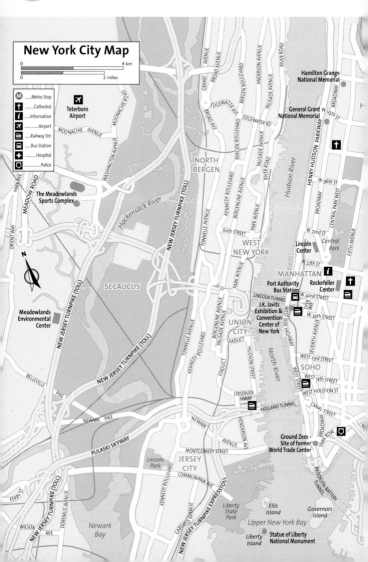

New York City Map

0   4 km
0   2 miles

M .....Metro Stop
✝ .....Cathedral
i .....Information
✈ .....Airport
🚃 .....Railway Stn
🚌 .....Bus Station
✚ .....Hospital
👮 .....Police

✈ Teterboro Airport

Hamilton Grange
National Memorial

General Grant
National Memorial

W. 125TH ST

BROADWAY

HENRY HUDSON PARKWAY

✝

W. 96th ST

CENTRAL PARK WEST

The Meadowlands
Sports Complex

EDGEWATER AVE

EDGEWATER RD

NORTH
BERGEN

Hudson River

KENNEDY BOULEVARD

BERGENLINE AVENUE

PARK AVENUE

PALISADE AVENUE

RIVER AVENUE

60th STREET

WEST
NEW YORK

BROADWAY

W. 72nd ST

Central
Park

Lincoln
Center

W. 57th ST

FIFTH AVENUE

MANHATTAN i

Port Authority
Bus Station

Rockefeller
Center

✝

Meadowlands
Environmental
Center

SECAUCUS

NEW JERSEY TURNPIKE (TOLL)

TONNELLE AVENUE

PARK AVENUE

32 ST

LINCOLN TUNNEL

LINCOLN TUNNEL

W. 42nd STREET

J.K. Javits
Exhibition &
Convention
Center of
New York

W. 34th STREET

NINTH AVENUE

SEVENTH AVENUE

WEST 23RD STREET

UNION
CITY

BERGENLINE AVENUE

PALISADE AVENUE

HUDSON STREET

VIADUCT

North River

WEST SIDE HIGHWAY

SOHO

WEST 14th STREET

WEST HOUSTON ST

BELLEVILLE   PIKE

NEW JERSEY TURNPIKE (TOLL)

KENNEDY BOULEVARD

TONNELLE AVENUE

VIADUCT

OBSERVER
HWAY

HOLLAND TUNNEL

CANAL STREET

BROADWAY

NEWARK   PIKE

N. EWARK

HENDERSON ST

AVENUE

Ground Zero -
Site of former
World Trade Center

PARK ROW

BROOKLYN-BATTERY TUNNEL

PULASKI SKYWAY

MONTGOMERY STREET

Lincoln
Park

JERSEY
CITY

COMMUNIPAW AVE

NEW JERSEY TURNPIKE EXPRESSTOLL

FERRY ST

NEW JERSEY TURNPIKE (TOLL)

WILSON

AVE

DOREMUS AVENUE

Newark
Bay

KENNEDY BOULEVARD

CARDIFO AVENUE

Liberty
State
Park

Ellis
Island

Governors
Island

Upper New York Bay

Liberty
Island

Statue of Liberty
National Monument

MEADOW ROAD

ORIENT WAY

GRAND AVENUE

BROAD AVENUE

BERGEN BOULEVARD

ANDERSON AVENUE

PALISADE AVENUE

RIVER ROAD

EDGEWATER AVE

MOONACHIE

MOONACHIE AVENUE

WASHINGTON AVENUE

Hackensack River

BROAD AVE

neighbourhood. You will immediately have a sense of the city's bustling crowds, beautiful buildings, and delectable shops.

Have a coffee while perusing city maps, and start to act like a New Yorker. Make a day's plan; leave maps tucked away well out of sight, and walk with a sense of purpose. The city is safer now than just a few years before, however, as in most large cities, be cautious at night – avoid being alone in unfamiliar dark places, or in parks. Look *both* ways before crossing any street; some are two way.

ORIENTATION

The island of Manhattan has such a wealth of sights that many visitors don't realise it is only one of five boroughs that belong to New York City. In fact, it is the smallest in size – 21 km (13 miles) long, and only 4 km (2.3 miles) wide – but literally packed with attractions. Brooklyn and the other boroughs, as well as New Jersey, are linked to Manhattan by many bridges, tunnels and ferries.

Fifth Avenue is the dividing line between East and West for street addresses. Building numbers increase with distance away from Fifth Avenue, about 100 per block. There is a dozen north/south major avenues numbered First Avenue to Twelfth Avenue (a few have names such as Lexington, Park, Madison, Broadway). Avenue of the Americas is the formal name for what everyone calls Sixth Avenue. Approximately 12 north–south blocks equal 1 kilometre (20 blocks to a mile). Most streets are one way; traffic travels in both directions on some wide streets such as 14th, 23rd, 34th, 42nd, 57th, 72nd, 86th, to name a few. Conveniently, most subway stations are located on these same streets; subway lines are INT, BMT and IRT.

From Greenwich Village northwards, the city is primarily a grid, so it is nearly impossible to get lost. The words Uptown and Downtown usually refer to the Upper East or Upper West bordering

Central Park. In the subway system, (or even if you are walking), Downtown and Uptown refer to the direction from where you are to where you are going – if you are travelling from 59th Street to 34th Street, you would be going Downtown. To find east/west cross streets for an Avenue address, use the **NYC Street Finder** (ⓦ www.nycvisit.com).

ⓘ CitySpots maps indicate main streets and sights. Below 14th Street and throughout the lower part of Manhattan, things can get messy.

⬤ *Look out for impressive mural art*

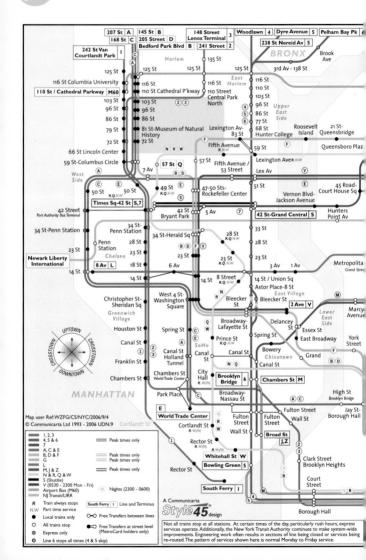

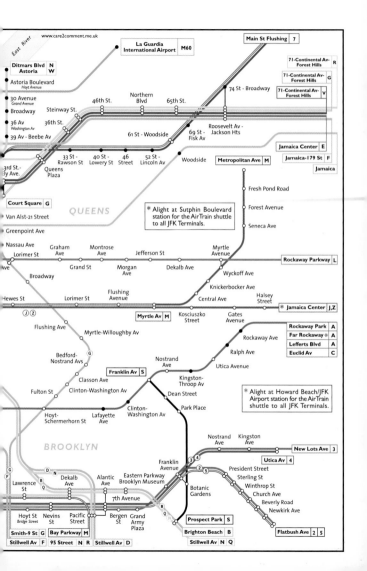

East River www.care2comment.me.uk

La Guardia International Airport M60

Main St Flushing 7

Ditmars Blvd N
Astoria W
Hoyt Avenue

71-Continental Av-
Forest Hills R

71-Continental Av-
Forest Hills G

Astoria Boulevard
Hoyt Avenue

74 St - Broadway

71-Continental Av-
Forest Hills V

30 Avenue
Grand Avenue

Northern
Blvd

46th St.

65th St.

Broadway

Steinway St.

36 Av
Washington Av

36th St.

61 St - Woodside

69 St -
Fisk Av

Roosevelt Av -
Jackson Hts

Jamaica Center E

39 Av - Beebe Av

Jamaica-179 St F

3rd St. -
ly Ave.

33 St -
Rawson St

40 St -
Lowery St

46
Street

52 St -
Lincoln Av

Woodside

Metropolitan Ave M

Jamaica

Queens
Plaza

Court Square G

QUEENS

Fresh Pond Road

Van Alst-21 Street

Forest Avenue

* Alight at Sutphin Boulevard
station for the AirTrain shuttle
to all JFK Terminals.

Seneca Ave

Greenpoint Ave

Nassau Ave

Graham
Ave

Montrose
Ave

Lorimer St

Jefferson St

Myrtle
Avenue

Rockaway Parkway L

ve.

Broadway

Grand St

Morgan
Ave

Dekalb Ave

Wyckoff Ave

Hewes St

Lorimer St

Flushing
Avenue

Knickerbocker Ave

Central Ave

Halsey
Street

* Jamaica Center J,Z

J 2

Flushing Avenue

Myrtle-Willoughby Av

Myrtle Av M

Kosciuszko
Street

Gates
Avenue

Rockaway Park A

Far Rockaway * A

Rockaway Ave

Lefferts Blvd A

Bedford-
Nostrand Avs

G

Nostrand
Ave

Ralph Ave

Euclid Av C

Franklin Av S

Classon Ave

Kingston-
Throop Av

Utica Avenue

Fulton St

Clinton-Washington Av

Dean Street

* Alight at Howard Beach/JFK
Airport station for the AirTrain
shuttle to all JFK Terminals.

Hoyt-
Schermerhorn St

Lafayette
Ave

Clinton-
Washington Av

Park Place

BROOKLYN

Nostrand
Ave

Kingston
Ave

New Lots Ave 3

G
F

D
Lawrence
St

N
Q

Dekalb
Ave

Atlantic
Ave

Franklin
Avenue

Eastern Parkway
Brooklyn Museum

3 4

President Street

Utica Av 4

7th Avenue

2 5

Sterling St

Winthrop St

Botanic
Gardens

Church Ave

B
Hoyt St
Bridge Street

Nevins
St

Pacific
Street

Bergen
St

Grand
Army
Plaza

Q

Beverly Road

Newkirk Ave

Smith-9 St G

Bay Parkway M

Prospect Park S

Flatbush Ave 2 5

Stillwell Av F

95 Street N R

Stillwell Av D

Brighton Beach B

Stillwell Av N Q

GETTING AROUND

Most people get around the city by bus or subway at $2/£1 per ride regardless of distance – use exact change in coins, a token, or a **MetroCard** (Ⓦ www.mta.info/metrocard), which permits transfers between buses and subways within two hours of purchase. MetroCards are found at newsstands, tobacco shops, some subway stations and hotels. Multiple ride MetroCards permit hop-on, hop-off travel. Subway rides are fast; buses are handy for short trips and good for the sightseeing, but they can be slow in traffic. The MetroCard includes some museum discounts, too.

During a short stay, it's wise to plan carefully how to navigate through the city, in order to see as much as possible. While at the **New York City Official Visitor Information Center** (ⓘ 212 New York Ⓦ www.nycvisit.com), buy a **CityPass** $53 (Ⓦ www.citypass.com) or MetroCard. Book a red double-decker London-style **Gray Line** bus tour (Ⓦ www.newyorksightseeing.com); there are 50 stops in Manhattan and Brooklyn. A 48-hour ticket costs about $48/£26 and permits hop-on, hop-off travel on three tour loops, from 08.00 to 17.00.

Yellow coloured metered **taxis** (also called 'cabs') are everywhere and can be hailed from the street. Available taxis travel with a roof-top number lit, but they won't stop for customers if the sign's 'Off Duty' portion is lit.

▶ *Lower East Side street market*

Midtown Manhattan

No one questions that midtown is the epitome of New York, and its heart is fervently beating here, among the skyscrapers and mass of people. Once farmland, and now a city, the people who work here among all the stone, cement and glass provide New York with its fruit. Photographs of the New York skyline are iconic, but midtown Manhattan comes to mind when someone says 'New York' or simply 'The City': skyscrapers stand tall like stalks of asparagus in a corded bunch; many of the top sightseeing attractions are within walking distance of each other; and there is a mecca of grand hotels and cosmopolitan shops. Despite cold weather, Christmas in New York warms the spirit, and is a wonderful time to visit. Lights twinkle in all the plazas, roasted chestnuts are sold on street corners, and shop windows become fairy tales.

Midtown runs along Fifth Avenue from 34th to 59th Streets, and east to the East River and west to the Hudson River. Numbered streets and avenues make getting around New York very easy. Everything is on the move here, people, cabs, trucks, bikes and buses. However, traffic gets completely snarled from Central Park all the way down to the Empire State building. Midtown gives total immersion into urban living. Stop to see famous statues, such as Atlas holding an art deco world, or watch a mime performer on any corner, with cars honking horns as the background music.

SIGHTS & ATTRACTIONS

Chrysler Building
Resembling a car topped with hubcap-style gargoyles, the art deco building is a distinctive city landmark. An impressive mural in the

lobby screams Fred Astaire and Ginger Rogers.

🅰 405 Lexington Avenue Ⓝ Subway: 4, 5, 6, 7 to Grand Central Station

Empire State Building

The art deco building's size, at 102 floors and 381 m (1,250 feet) high, made it the tallest skyscraper in the world when it was built in 1931. It held that record for over 40 years, until the World Trade Center was finished. Thrilling panoramic views are seen from the observation tower, including many city landmarks. When it's windy, you can feel the building sway. Queues can be long; purchase tickets online, or buy a CityPass in advance.

🅰 350 Fifth Avenue Ⓦ www.esbnyc.com 🕐 08.00–24.00 Ⓝ Subway: A, C, E, 1, 2, 3 to 34th Street–Penn Station; B, D, F, N, Q, R to 34th Street–Herald Square

Ford Foundation Atrium

The world's first atrium is inside the Ford Foundation. The interior garden is surrounded by offices. It's surprising to see this lush, green retreat, complete with a lily pond and trees, in an urban setting. It was built by Roche Dinkeloo for America's largest philanthropic organisation.

🅰 320 E 43rd Street 🕿 212 573 5000 🕐 09.00–17.00 Mon–Fri, closed Sat & Sun Ⓝ Subway: S, 4, 5, 6, 7 to 42nd Street

Grand Army Plaza

The postcard scene of horse-drawn carriages in this beautiful plaza with its Pulitzer Fountain and a statue of Pomona, the Roman

---

▶ *The Empire State Building says it all*

goddess of abundance, is a focal point of the midtown area. Whether heading into the Park or on your way down Fifth Avenue, this is a wide open space to stop and catch your breath, and to do a little people-watching.

🅐 59th Street and Fifth Avenue Ⓝ Subway: N, R, 4, 5, 6 to 59th Street, F to 57th Street

Great White Way (Broadway) & Times Square

Two huge avenues converge to make the triangle known as Times Square. As dusk settles in, the lights on theatre marquees and giant billboards light up with an intoxicating brilliance, giving this stretch of Broadway its nickname. Thousands of revellers gather here on New Year's Eve to see the ball drop, while another billion people watch on television. A collection of theatres lines the side streets west of Times Square; like almost everything else, theatre inched its way uptown from the Bowery to 42nd Street. From Vaudeville and the Ziegfeld Follies, through great stars like the Marx Brothers, to the ultimate of sleaze in the 1970s and 1980s, the Great White Way is now in a dazzling, new era. Old theatres have been restored, and new ones share the street with Disney® and Toys "Я" Us. Take a walk, or see a show – in the triangle where the neon never dims.

🅐 1 Times Square Ⓦ www.timessquare.com Ⓝ Subway: N, Q, R, S, 1, 2, 3, 7 to 42nd Street–Times Square

Rockefeller Center

A sloping path through the Channel Gardens leads to Rockefeller Center's sunken plaza, surrounded by international flags and the rink where skaters dance across the ice. The gardens are decorated

◀ *The Chrysler Building, built in the art deco style*

each season, and especially at Christmas when an enormous Norway Spruce Christmas tree is lit. The Center is an outdoor art deco museum, with its beautiful 1930s buildings, and many sculptures, including the prominent *Prometheus* that presides over the rink. More than 20 buildings are linked by an underground concourse, unofficially called the 'Catacombs', and within is a myriad of shops and eateries. You can grab a lunch-to-go, and picnic near the gardens, or settle in at the Rock Center Café to watch the skaters and have a leisurely meal.

ⓐ Rockefeller Center ☎ 212 664 3700 ⓦ www.rockefellercenter.com
Ⓝ Subway: F, D, B, to Rockefeller Center, 6 to 51st Street–Lexington Avenue, 1 to 50th Street–Broadway, N, R to 49th Street **NBC Studio Tour** ☎ 212 664 7174 🕘 08.30–17.30 Mon–Sat, 09.30–16.30 Sun **Ice-Skating Rink** ☎ 212 332 7654 ⓦ www.rapatina.com

St Patrick's Cathedral

The lofty spires of the decorated Gothic-style Catholic Cathedral pierce the air over Fifth Avenue. Walk inside to see its impressive size, beautiful stained-glass windows, and a giant organ. The Cathedral holds 2,200 people and is the seat of the Archdiocese of New York.

ⓐ 51st Street and Fifth Avenue ☎ 212 753 2261
ⓦ www.ny-archdiocese.org 🕘 06.30–20.45 Ⓝ Subway: B, D, F, V to 47/50th Street

Top of the Rock™

Designed with an ocean liner theme, the Observation Deck has recently opened after two decades for visitors to enjoy its 70th-floor views and the sparkling lights of the city and beyond. Reserved tickets only, which is a good way to avoid queues.

ⓐ 30 Rockefeller Center ⓣ 212 698 2000

ⓦ www.topoftherocknyc.com ⓛ 08.30–24.00 ⓝ Subway: B, D, F, V
to 47/50th Street–Rockefeller Center, N, R, W to 49th St–Seventh
Avenue, E, V to 53rd Street–Fifth Avenue, 6 to E 51st Street–Lexington
Avenue, 1, 9 to 50th Street–Broadway

United Nations

The flags of all its member nations wave outside this large complex
devoted to the preservation of worldwide peace and security. Tours
include a visit to the Security Council, the domed General Assembly
Hall, and artworks throughout.

ⓐ Visitor's entrance 46th Street and First Avenue ⓣ 212 963 8687

ⓦ www.un.org ⓛ 09.30–16.45 Mon–Fri, 10.00–16.30 Sat & Sun

ⓝ Subway: 4, 5, 6, 7 to 42nd Street–Grand Central Station

CULTURE

Midtown has its share of museums, but it's the MoMA (Museum of
Modern Art) that everyone comes to see. Smaller museums of note
are the American Folk Art Museum, the International Center of
Photography, and the Intrepid Sea-Air Space Museum.

Carnegie Hall

There's nothing quite like being in this acoustically perfect hall for a
big concert, packed 2,800 strong with an enthusiastic crowd. The
programme includes many music genres from hot jazz and soloists
to classical orchestras.

ⓐ 54 West 57th Street ⓣ 212 903 9765 ⓦ www.carnegiehall.org

ⓛ Tours: 11.30, 14.00, 15.00 Mon–Fri ⓝ Subway: A, B, C, D, 1 to
Columbus Circle, E, N, Q, R, W to 57th Street–Seventh Avenue

Culture on the Run

It's not a 'place', it's a 'happening'. Subway music used to be an impromptu thing – a lone trumpeter playing soul music. Nowadays, 'Music Under New York' is played regularly in subway stations at Times Square, Columbus Circle, Rockefeller Center, Union Square, Borough Hall, and Grand Army Plaza in Brooklyn, and at all railway stations. And that's not all; the Metropolitan Transportation Authority (MTA; Ⓦ www.mta.nyc.ny.us) installs permanent artwork in renovated stations, plus annual posters, and *Poetry in Motion*.

🔺 *Prometheus looks over the courtyard of the Rockefeller Center*

Museum of Modern Art (MoMA)

A walk through the MoMA is like taking a walk through the 20th century of modern art. Here you can gaze on real-life originals of images that have been seen over and over again in books and magazines. Room after room is filled with great paintings such as Cezanne's *The Bather* and Van Gogh's *The Starry Night*. Also represented are earthy Gaugin paintings, cubist era paintings of Pablo Picasso, and Monet's *Lily Ponds*. There's the surrealism of Dalí, and colour-splashed canvasses by Jackson Pollack and Mark Rothko. There's a Sculpture Garden, and a huge collection of photography.
🄰 11 W 53rd Street 🄣 212 708 9400 🅦 www.moma.org 🄻 10.30–17.30 Sat–Mon, Wed & Thur, 10.30–20.00 Fri, closed Tues 🄼 Subway: E or V to 53rd Street–Fifth Avenue, B, D, F to 47–50th Streets–Rockefeller Center

Pierpont Morgan Library

This delightful small museum, set in a quiet neighbourhood, houses rare manuscripts and priceless works by authors Mark Twain and Lewis Carroll. 🄰 29 E 36th Street 🄣 212 590 0300 🅦 www.morganlibrary.org 🄻 10.30–17.00 Tues–Thur, until 20.00 Fri, until 18.00 Sat & Sun, closed Mon 🄼 Subway: D, F to 34th Street, 4, 5, 6 to 33rd Street

RETAIL THERAPY

Fifth Avenue is a long shopping centre, and creatively designed shop windows are its trademark. You'll stroll by great designer shops like Gucci and Armani, or chic department stores like Bergdorf Goodman, or the Japanese store, Takashimaya. Jewellers who sell baubles to celebrities and billionaires are here, too – Bulgari, and the House of Harry Winston, for example. Rockefeller Center alone is filled with shops from Banana Republic to Barnes and Noble. You can also repair a watch there, or get your shoes shined. Many shops are open on Sundays. If you need a brief respite, slip into Paley's Vest Pocket Park on E 53rd Street.

The Diamond District A single street is devoted to jewellery and diamonds, where you can probably find a nice rock at wholesale prices – if buying, be sure to compare. All along W 47th Street, west of Fifth Avenue, Hasidic dealers wheel and deal in close quarters, among 2,600 shops. ☎ 212 302 5739 ⓦ www.diamonddistrict.org ⏰ Most shops 10.00–17.00 Mon–Fri ⓝ Subway: see Rockefeller Center (page 63)

FAO Schwarz Spend some time shopping in this engaging emporium of toys, and you'll feel like a child again. Hug soft lush teddy bears to your heart, hop out a tune on the larger-than-life Dance-On-Piano, and don't leave without stopping at FAO Schweetz for a towering milkshake or frosty ice cream float. ⓐ 767 Fifth Avenue ☎ 212 644 9400 ⏰ 10.00–19.00 Mon–Sat, 11.00–18.00 Sun ⓝ Subway: N, R, W to 59th Street–Fifth Avenue, 4, 5, 6 to 59th Street–Lexington Avenue

Macy's Often called the 'Miracle of 34th Street' this is the city's largest, block-long department store, an amazing place that sells everything from cosmetics and clothes to food delicacies and household goods. There's even a free personalised shopping service. ⓐ 151 W 34th Street ☎ 212 695 4400 ⓦ www.macys.com ⏰ 10.00–20.30 Mon–Sat, 11.00–19.00 Sun ⓝ Subway: B, D, F, N, Q, R at 34th Street

Tiffany & Co Taking home 'anything' wrapped in the trademark blue box, tied with a white satin ribbon, is symbolic of buying elegance. You can find little treasures at Tiffany's for under $100/£53. 🅐 727 Fifth Avenue 🕐 212 755 8000 🅦 www.tiffany.com 🕐 10.00–19.00 Mon–Fri, until 18.00 Sat, 12.00–17.00 Sun 🅝 Subway: N, R, W to 59th Street–Fifth Avenue, 4, 5, 6 to 59th Street/Lexington Avenue

TAKING A BREAK

With all the hustle and bustle, you'll need a break. Slip over to the East River and ride the Tram to Roosevelt Island, or stroll through elegant Sutton Place. If you're now used to the crowds, picnic in Rockefeller Center.

Au Bon Pain £ ❶ Grab a sandwich or wrap, and people-watch in the plaza. 🅐 1211 Sixth Avenue 🕐 212 840 5093 🅦 www.aubonpain.com 🅝 Subway: see Rockefeller Center (page 63)

Ben & Jerry's £ ❷ Get a sugar boost with scrumptious Vermont ice cream. 🅐 30 Rockefeller Center 🕐 212 218 7843 🅦 www.benjerry.com 🅝 Subway: see Rockefeller Center (page 63)

Dean & Deluca £ ❸ Another picnic ingredients spot; get some delicacies to munch lunch on here. 🅐 9 Rockefeller Plaza 🕐 212 664 1363 🅦 www.deananddeluca.com 🅝 Subway: see Rockefeller Center (page 63)

Oyster Bar & Restaurant ££ ❹ Under an impressive curved and tiled ceiling, and purportedly 'below sea level', gulp down some super-fresh Long Island Blue Points in the Oyster Bar.

Before you leave, take time to marvel at the restored cathedral ceiling – a night sky with stars and constellations. ⓐ Grand Central Station ⓘ 212 490 6650 ⓦ www.oysterbarny.com ⓛ 11.30–21.30 Mon–Fri, 12.00–21.30 Sat, closed Sun ⓝ Subway: S, 4, 5, 6, 7 to 42nd Street–Grand Central Station

Rock Center Café ££ ❺   Watch the ice skating while lunching in style. ⓐ 20 W 50th Street ⓘ 212 332 7620 ⓦ www.rapatina.com ⓝ Subway: see Rockefeller Center (page 63)

Algonquin Hotel ££–£££ ❻   Stop for a drink in the famous Rose Room Bar and soak up the literary atmosphere. Noel Coward and George Bernard Shaw are among the theatrical celebrities who stayed at the Hotel. ⓐ 59 W 44th Street ⓘ 212 840 6800 ⓦ www.algonquinhotel.com ⓝ Subway: B, D, F, V at 42nd Street

AFTER DARK

If you want to see real stars, take a ride to the top of the Marriot Marquis in Times Square to The View, New York's only revolving rooftop restaurant. Some of New York's best restaurants are in midtown; save some money to try one.

Restaurants
Carnegie Deli ££ ❼   This quintessential New York Jewish deli is seen in Woody Allen's movie, *Broadway Danny Rose*. It's famous for gigantic heart-attack sandwiches filled with corned beef, pastrami brisket and chopped liver. Oh yes, and try the cheesecake.

◀ *Join the crowds at the Rockefeller Center*

📍 854 Seventh Avenue 📞 212 757 2245 🌐 www.carnegiedeli.com
🕐 06.30–04.00 Mon–Sun Ⓜ Subway: B, D, E, to Seventh Avenue, N, R
to 57th Street

Aureole £££ **8** Situated in a Brownstone building, with rooms full
of fresh flowers, you can experience Charlie Palmer's progressive
American cuisine, and the flavourful meals prepared by Chef Dante
Boccuzzi. On a budget? Try the *prix fixe* menu 📍 34 E 61st Street
📞 212 319 1660 🌐 www.charliepalmer.com 🕐 12.00–14.30,
17.30–23.00 Mon–Fri, 17.00–23.00 Sat, closed Sun Ⓜ Subway: N, R, W
to 59th Street–Lexington Avenue

Le Bernardin £££ **9** The creation of Chef Eric Ripert, this is toted as
one of New York's best restaurants. Seafood is cooked to perfection
with a French accent, topped with delicacies like sea urchin or
truffles. There are some tasting menus that help bring down the
expense of trying out a restaurant of this calibre. 📍 155 W 51st Street
📞 212 489 1515 🌐 www.le-bernardin.com 🕐 12.00–14.30 Mon–Fri,
17.30–22.30 Mon–Thur, until 23.00 Fri & Sat, closed Sun Ⓜ Subway:
B, D, F, V to 47th–50th Streets–Rockefeller Center

Four Seasons £££ **10** The stunning Pool Room is graced by a
tranquil marble pool surrounded by dinner tables, and floor-to-
ceiling windows covered with undulating metal curtains, a lovely
setting for a romantic evening. The Grill Room is a power-lunch
scene. Modern art in the restaurant includes a Picasso stage curtain,
and several Lichtenstein lithographs. 📍 99 E 52nd Street 📞 212 754
9494 🕐 12.00–14.00, 17.00–21.30 Mon–Fri, 17.00–23.15 Sat, closed Sun
Ⓜ Subway: 6 to 51st Street, E, V to 53rd Street–Lexington Avenue

The Rainbow Room £££ ⓫ Tea-dance to Big Band ballroom music, surrounded by sparkling city lights from this 65th floor perch. ⓐ Rockefeller Plaza ⓣ 212 632 5000 ⓛ 17.00–23.30 Mon–Sun ⓦ www.rainbowroom.com ⓝ Subway: see Rockefeller Center (page 63)

Cinemas & theatres
Radio City Music Hall Since its opening, the Rockettes have thrilled audiences with their leggy precision and high-kick dance. They perform at the Christmas Spectacular and Easter Show. The art deco interior is worth the ticket price simply to experience the sheer size of the 5,874-seat theatre, and its scallop shell stage. ⓐ 1260 Sixth Avenue ⓣ 212 307 7171 ⓦ www.radiocity.com ⓝ Subway: see Rockefeller Center (page 63)

Bars, clubs & discos
P J Clarke's This tenacious little saloon has been around since the mid 1800s, 'holding out' when developers built a 45-storey building behind it. After a renovation and a few menu additions, the juicy cheeseburgers are still its prize dish. Crooners like Frank Sinatra and Nat King Cole enjoyed the saloon's casual atmosphere. ⓐ 915 Third Avenue ⓣ 212 317 1616 ⓦ www.pjclarkes.com ⓛ 11.30–04.00 ⓝ Subway: E, V to Lexington Avenue, 4, 5, 6, F, N, R, W to 59th Street, 6 to 51st Street

Wall Street & Chinatown

A belt of green wraps around the thumb-tip of Manhattan, full of small idyllic picnic spots with views over the harbour to the Statue of Liberty. It's hardly a harbinger of the frenetic activity around Wall Street, just a few blocks north. Long ago, downtown was the city's heart and soul and, ever so briefly, the country's capital. Then, downtown ended abruptly at City Hall, with only farmland beyond. City Hall's northern façade was even left unfinished as no one would see it, and no one imagined the future northward exodus into the farmland areas. Just beyond City Hall are courthouses, at the edge of Chinatown and Little Italy.

SIGHTS & ATTRACTIONS

Nearly every corner took part in the city's history, so it's best to walk, but the free Downtown Connection bus helps when feet get tired. Most of New York's oldest and impressive buildings are here – Trinity Church and the graveyard where Alexander Hamilton rests, the Woolworth Building's gilded hall, and Broadway's *Canyon of Heroes*, where ticker tape parades celebrate heroes.

African Burial Ground National Monument

The remains of 419 Africans were discovered in 1991 during pre-construction of a federal building, now a permanent memorial to 20,000 colonial-era enslaved Africans who rest here. ⓐ Interpretive Center adjacent to the site 290 Broadway (burial ground on Duane Street) ⓣ 212 637 2039 ⓦ www.africanburialground.com ⓒ 09.00–16.00 Mon–Fri, closed

Wall Street & Chinatown

0	500 metres
0	500 yards

Pier 32

N.Y.C. Fire Museum

Spring Street

Spring St

SOHO

BROOME ST

LITTLE ITALY

HUDSON SQUARE

GRAND ST

CANAL STREET

TRIBECA

CHINA TOWN

BAYARD ST

Museum of Chinese in the Americas

Columbus Park

CANAL STREET

African Burial Ground National Monument

WORTH STREET

DUANE STREET

City Hall

FULTON

Pier 21

Chambers St

WTC

Brooklyn Br

BROOKLYN BRIDGE

MURRAY STREET

Park Pl

BARCLAY STREET

St Paul's Chapel

Fulton St

Pier 26
Pier 25

BATTERY PARK CITY

North Cove

Ground Zero - Site of former World Trade Center

South Street Seaport Museum

LIBERTY STREET

Federal Reserve Bank

Exhibition of Historic Vessels

Pier 14

New York Stock Exchange

Federal Hall

FINANCIAL DISTRICT

ALBANY ST

RECTOR PLACE

National Museum of the American Indian

Skyscraper Museum

Fraunces Tavern Museum

Pier 9

Robert F. Wagner Jr. Park

Battery Park

Bowling Green

Pier 6

Castle Clinton National Monument

South Ferry

Staten Island Ferry Terminal

BROOKLYN - BATTERY TUNNEL (TOLL)

Hudson River

Liberty State Park

Immigration Museum

ELLIS ISLAND

Statue of Liberty / National Monument

US Coast Guard Station, New York

GOVERNORS ISLAND

Ⓜ	Metro Stop
✝	Cathedral
ℹ	Information
✈	Airport
🚉	Railway Stn
✚	Hospital
Ⓟ	Police

Sat & Sun Subway: N, Q, R, W to Canal Street, J, M, Z to Chambers Street, 4, 5, 6 to Brooklyn Bridge–City Hall.

Battery Park

Among several memorials and statues is *The Sphere*, a remnant of the grand sculpture salvaged from the WTC Plaza (temporary installation www.thebattery.org). **Castle Clinton National Monument**, the fort that never fired a shot, spent a varied life as a restaurant, then an opera venue, later a gateway for immigrants, and an aquarium. The fort is open for tours Bowling Green and State Street www.nps.gov/cacl 08.00–17.00 Subway: R, W to Whitehall Street, 1 to South Ferry, 4, 5 to Bowling Green

Federal Reserve Bank

Billions of dollars worth of glittering gold bullion are stored 15 m (50 ft) below sea level in the bank vaults of this magnificent neo-Renaissance building. To see the stash by guided tour (every half hour on the hour), advance reservations are required at least a week before; call first for availability or email requests to frbnytours@ny.frb.org 33 Liberty Street 212 720 6130 www.newyorkfed.org 09.30–11.30, 13.30–14.30 Mon–Fri, closed Sat & Sun Subway: 2, 3, 4, 5 to Wall Street

Ground Zero

A high fence surrounds the mournful remains of the World Trade Center, where lofty twin towers once gloriously and symbolically defined the downtown area. Construction is progressing on the museum, performing arts centre, and the 541 m (1776 ft) tall Freedom Tower – its height in feet references the year of independence. It's worth taking a peek through the fence;

the grim reminder of a horrible time is gripping. Santiago Calatrava's exciting bird-in-flight transportation hub is also on the horizon.

ⓐ Located in a rectangle spanning from West Street to Church Street and Liberty Street to Vesey Street ⓝ Subway: A, C, E, J, M, Z, 1, 2 to Chambers Street, N, R to City Hall, 4, 5, 6 to Brooklyn Bridge–City Hall

South Street Seaport

The four-mast *Peking* is just one of the barques alongside the piers in South Street Seaport – an 11-square-block historic district. This complex is full of shops, cafés, and has a fish market. Museum ⓐ 19 Fulton Street ⓣ 212 748 8600 ⓦ www.southstseaport.org ⓛ 10.00–16.00 Tues–Sun, closed Mon (summer); 10.00–17.00 Fri–Mon, closed Tues–Thur (winter) ⓝ Subway: A, C to Broadway–Nassau, 2, 3, 4, 5, J, Z, M to Fulton Street, A, C to Broadway–Nassau

St Paul's Chapel

The oldest church in Manhattan, St Paul's is where George Washington prayed under the Waterford glass chandeliers during his first presidential term. Located directly across from the World Trade Center, it quickly became the centre of an enormous volunteer relief effort after the 11 September 2001 attacks. See the exhibit *Unwavering Spirit: Hope & Healing* at Ground Zero.

ⓐ 209 Broadway ⓣ 212 233 4164 www.saintpaulschapel.org ⓝ Subway: E to Chambers Street, R to Cortlandt Street, 1, 9, 4, 5 and A to Fulton Street–Broadway–Nassau, 6 to Brooklyn Bridge–City Hall

Staten Island Ferry

With spanking new terminals on both ends of the trip, the ferry to Staten Island is the best freebie in New York. Each year, 19 million people take this veritable cruise for 8 km (5.2 miles), passing close by Ellis Island and Lady Liberty. Time this trip for a glorious sunset, with postcard views of Manhattan and its bridges.

ⓐ Whitehall Terminal, 1 Whitehall Street ⓣ 718 815 2628
ⓦ www.si-web.com/SI-Ferry.html ⓞ Daily, about every half hour, 24 hours a day ⓢ Subway: 1, 9 to South Ferry, 4, 5 to Bowling Green, N, R to Whitehall Street

🔺 New York's most famous landmark, the Statue of Liberty

Statue of Liberty/Ellis Island Immigration Museum National Monument

The statue, created by sculptor Frederic Auguste Barthodi, is a gift from the people of France, honouring the 100-year anniversary of America's independence. It sits on Bedloe Island in New York Harbor, and is now a universal symbol of freedom and democracy. The poem by Emma Lazarus that graces its base, *The New Colossus*, is very well known – 'Give me your tired, your poor, your huddled masses yearning to breathe free...'

Ellis Island From 1892 to 1924, more than 22 million immigrants, passengers and crew members came through Ellis Island and the Port of New York. The main building has been a museum since 1990.

ⓐ New York Harbor (reached by ferry) ☎ 212 363 3200; ferry 212 269 5755 ⓦ www.nps.gov/stli ⓝ Ferry runs every 25 minutes 08.30–15.00 (some seasonal variation); Subway: R to Whitehall Street, 1 to South Ferry, 4, 5 to Bowling Green, then take the Statue of Liberty Ferry from the southern part of Battery Park

Wall Street

Since 9/11, Wall Street has been a pedestrian way, which suits this narrow street where George Washington was inaugurated as America's first president in 1789. The spot is marked by his statue in front of **Federal Hall National Monument**. The current building was a Customs House, then a treasury vault. The **New York Stock Exchange** is dressed in tall Corinthian columns. In pre-9/11 days, one could watch a flurry of activity on the trading floor, where $5 trillion is traded each year. Unfortunately, the Visitor's Gallery is now closed.

Federal Hall ⓐ 26 Wall Street ☎ 212 825 6888 ⓦ www.nps.gov/feha ⏱ 09.00–17.00 Mon–Fri, closed Sat & Sun;

New York Stock Exchange 20 Broad Street www.nyse.com
 Subway: 4, 5 to Wall Street, J, M, Z to Broad Street

CULTURE

Except for Fraunces Tavern, one of the few buildings in Manhattan
that actually bore witness to the American Revolution, most of the
museums in the financial district are fairly new.

Fraunces Tavern Museum

The Tavern, as the oldest building in Manhattan, recalls popular
tales from colonial times. The restaurant serves continental fare,
but its history is the big attraction. George Washington bid
farewell to his officers here in 1783, at a victory banquet in the Long
Room, after a grisly Revolutionary war. The museum not only has a
lock of Washington's hair, but it also has one of his false teeth!
 54 Pearl Street 212 425 1778 www.fraruncestavernmuseum.org
 12.00–17.00 Tues–Fri, 10.00–17.00 Sat, closed Sun & Mon
 Subway: J, M, Z to Broad Street, 4, 5 to Bowling Green

Museum of Chinese in the Americas

Two small rooms shaped like a Chinese lantern contain exhibits
concerning Chinese life in America; the museum includes poignant
family histories handed down from 'old-timers'.
 70 Mulberry Street, 2nd floor 212 619 4785 www.moca-nyc.org
 12.00–17.00 Tues–Sun, closed Mon Subway: J, M, Z, N, Q, R, W, 6
to Canal Street

National Museum of the American Indian

The George Gustav Heye Center at Alexander Hamilton US Custom

House is certainly a long title, but befitting such a formidable place. The marble and granite beaux arts building itself is remarkable, with its 44 columns topped with the head of Mercury, and a dozen elegant statues above. Carvings, masks, pottery, Navajo weavings, Mayan carved jade and Andean gold are just part of the rich collection brought to this new museum from the Smithsonian Institute.

One Bowling Green 212 514 3700 www.nmai.si.edu

CHINATOWN

Mott Street is home to an enclave of Chinese immigrants. A two-week long, colourful festival celebrates Chinese New Year. Cymbals announce multi-coloured fabric-covered lion dancers. They wend their way through crowded streets with huge, bobbing, dragon-like heads and rolling eyes. Costumed men dance in tempo to drums and gongs. Firecrackers blast loudly to scare away evil beasts, and thousands throng the tiny streets to join the parade and festivity.

Chinatown is a maze of cobblestone streets filled with Chinese character signs, red pagoda-styled storefronts, and kitschy shops. Bargain hunters haggle over Canal Street designer knock-offs, while on Mott Street, savvy New Yorkers seek out herb medicines, exotic veggies, and fresh fish. Crowded restaurants dish up every imaginable Chinese recipe. The total bill is likely to be less than the tax paid in uptown eateries. Mott Street and Canal Street www.explorechinatown.com Subway: 6, J, M, N, Q, R, W, Z to Canal Street, B, D to Grand Street, F to East Broadway station

🕐 10.00–17.00 Mon–Wed & Fri–Sun, until 20.00 Thur Ⓝ Subway:
R, W to Whitehall Street, 1 to South Ferry, 4, 5 to Bowling Green

Skyscraper Museum
Dazzling contemporary architecture with a core exhibit
Skyscraper/City.
🅰 39 Battery Place ☎ 212 968 1961 🕐 12.00–18.00 Wed–Sun, closed
Mon & Tues Ⓝ Subway: 4, 5 to Bowling Green

❗ The best place to buy discount theatre tickets without a long
wait is at the TKTS booth in South Street Seaport.

TAKING A BREAK

Go to lofty heights and have a drink at the Rise Bar (on the
14th Floor for the Ritz Carlton), or cruise out into the harbour
for a breath of fresh air.

🔺 *Peking duck is a favourite in Chinatown's restaurants*

Chinatown Ice Cream Factory £ ❶ Chinese flavours are the specialty at this family-run ice-cream factory. How about an icy Wasabi on a hot day? ➋ 65 Bayard Street ➊ 212 608 4170 ⓦ www.chinatownicecreamfactory.com ➌ 11.00–22.00 ➍ Subway: N, R, Q, W, 6 to Canal Street

Cyber Cigar Coffee Bar £ ❷ Check your email over a Seattle coffee with pastry and – surprise! – premium hand-rolled cigars in the Seaport Mall. ➋ Pier 17, South Street Seaport ➊ 212 406 3886

AFTER DARK

In the past, when the Stock Exchange closing bell sounded at 16.00, the whole Wall Street area became a dark, deserted void. After 9/11, New York bounced back, and the downtown area took on a new life.

Restaurants

Congee Bowery Restaurant £ ❸ Flavourful Cantonese seafood, steamed seasonal fish, or fish maw with black bean sauce, sautéed sliced conch with chives, and congee, a rice soup porridge. ➋ 207 Bowery ➊ 212 766 2828 ⓦ www.congeevillage.com ➍ Subway: J, M, Z to Bowery, D to Grand Street, 6 to Spring Street

The 14 Wall Street Restaurant ££ ❹ Elegant dining the J P Morgan way. Try a winter *prix fixe* entrée of crispy trout pancetta, green lentils, cippolini and onions. ➋ 14 Wall Street ➊ 212 233 2780 ⓦ www.14wallstreetrestaurant.com ➌ 07.00–09.30 Tues–Sat, 11.30–14.30 & 17.00–20.00 Mon–Fri, closed Sat & Sun ➍ Subway: 4, 5 to Wall Street, J, M, Z to Broad Street

Upper East Side

New York's oil barons and steel magnates spared no expense when building their palatial pads on Fifth Avenue opposite Central Park. Movers and shakers abandoned Manhattan's tip, slowly inching their way uptown. They got all the way to Riverside Drive and Harlem and, in the process, they left behind Manhattan's most prestigious addresses in the Carnegie Hill neighbourhood. Andrew Carnegie referred to his 64-room mansion as 'modest'! Architecture on the avenue is exquisite, and the area is ferociously protected by its high-brow residents. Forget the subway; take a bus to sightsee along this beautiful stretch of the island.

SIGHTS & ATTRACTIONS

The whole Upper East Side has a genteel village ambiance with its tree-lined side streets and lovely old brownstone buildings. Central Park breathes fresh air on to the avenue where Jackie O' once dodged paparazzi, and that J P Getty called home.

Central Park

Not enough can be said about this huge emerald that glistens in the heart of the city. Take a walk in the park, join the march of strollers under a green canopy of trees, and hobnob with the rich and famous, or at least their *au pairs*. Stop to people-watch at Bethesda Terrace, or watch model boats cruise the pond close to E 72nd Street. Further down is the old-fashioned Carousel. Stop at the **Dairy** (❶ 212 794 6564) for park information or to buy a poster. ❶ 212 3603444 Ⓦ www.centralparknyc.org Ⓝ Bus: 1, 2, 3, 4 on Fifth Avenue; Subway: 4, 5, 6 trains

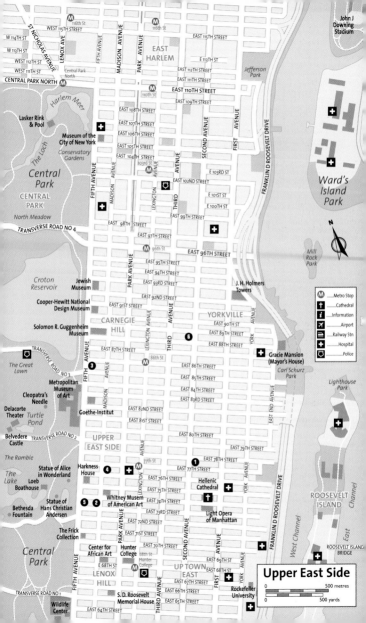

HIGH RISE HAWK

It's hard enough to get into one of the privileged and very pricey mansions on Fifth Avenue, but no one, that means *no one*, gets evicted. So it came as a big surprise to Pale Male, a red-tailed hawk, when he and partner, Lola, were ousted out of their precarious coop (pun intended) on the 12th story ledge of 927 Fifth, a co-op. Pale Male had been mating on his perch for a decade, under the careful watch of binocular-bearing bird lovers, and he gained celebrity status as the star of a movie, *Pale Male*, made possible by Frederic Lilien, who kept a six-year vigil on the hawk. Protesters, who included Mary Tyler Moore, dressed up as birds and waved placards, 'Honk for Hawks', and passing cabbies and bus drivers often complied. It all came to a peaceful resolution when building owners bowed to environmentalists and constructed a nesting platform. Pale Male returned to his perch, and he and Lola can sometimes be seen mating nearby on Woody Allen's balcony. Now, *there's* a New York story!

Wildlife Conservation Society's Central Park Zoo

Nobody's on a diet over at the Polar Zone where Gus and Ida prowl their rocky habitat for peanut-butter balls. These polar bears are experienced divers, too. Visit also the Tropic Zone, which houses a fantastic collection of tropical birds, and the Temperate Territory, which includes the California sealion tank. The sea lion quartet feeding (🕐 11.30, 14.00 & 16.00) is also popular.

☎ 212 439 6500 ⓦ www.centralpark.com 🕐 10.00–17.00 Mon–Fri, 10.00–17.30 Sat & Sun (Apr–end Oct); 10.00–16.30 (Nov–end Mar)
Ⓝ Bus: 1, 2, 3, 4 on Fifth Avenue; Subway: 4, 5, 6 trains

CULTURE

Philanthropic New Yorkers bequeathed their mansions and art collections to New York by establishing some of the world's most wonderful museums on Museum Mile. June visitors can attend the Festival held on the second Tuesday that month on Fifth Avenue from 82nd to 104th Street. Several other not-to-be-missed museums are also located in this area.

Cooper-Hewitt National Design Museum

Housed in Andrew Carnegie's 'modest' mansion, Cooper-Hewitt is an extension of the Smithsonian Institution. Its permanent collections explore both contemporary and historic design from graphics to decorative arts, with large exhibits of textiles, and even wallpaper. Some changing exhibits are sharp and cutting edge, others are presented with a sense of humour.

ⓐ 2 E 91st Street ☎ 212 849 8400 ⓦ www.cooperhewitt.org
🕐 10.00–17.00 Tues–Thur, until 21.00 Fri, until 18.00 Sat, 12.00–18.00 Sun, Tues free admission, closed Mon Ⓝ Subway: 4, 5, 6 to 86th Street

The Frick Collection

If you visit the Frick, as aficionados fondly call it, you'll immediately add it to your short list of favourite museums, mainly because it's small enough to see in a day, and the collection is the ultimate in high quality. Stroll through the elegant beaux art home relishing exquisite 18th-century French furniture, oriental rugs, porcelains and enamels. Get a sense of what it was like when Henry Clay Frick actually lived in this mansion, together with his old master European paintings. Relax a moment at the courtyard atrium, and

continue your journey through the 18 galleries, with some of the world's most famous paintings: Renoir's *Mother and Children*, Romney's *Lady Hamilton as 'Nature'*, or El Greco's magnificent red-robed *St Jerome*. The list is too long, but don't miss the old master European painters: Rembrandt, Titian, Gainsborough and Vermeer.
🄰 1 E 70th Street 🄣 212 288 0700 🅦 www.frick.org 🄲 10.00–18.00 Tues–Sat, 11.00–17.00 Sun, closed Mon 🄼 Subway: 6 to 68th Street/Hunter College

Metropolitan Museum of Art
The magnificent Met, as it is known to New Yorkers, has permanent collections representing every corner of the earth, and every era. The museum is so vast that you could explore the art here for several months (or years). Start at the reflecting pool in front of the Egyptian Nubian *Temple of Dendur* (circa 15BC), decorated with elegant sandstone reliefs (and some 19th-century graffiti!). The Met is organised in sections, easily reached from its neo-classical Great Hall. European masters are represented by El Greco's *View of Toledo*, or Titian's *Venus and the Lute Player*. The American collection is large and varied. The Met was a late-comer to modern art, but there is a healthy collection of works from Pablo Picasso to Jackson Pollack (see the Whitney and MoMa for larger modern collections). To satisfy hunger pangs, there are several cafés; be sure to view the skyline from the Roof Garden (open May to late autumn), or have cocktails and appetisers at the Balcony Bar while enjoying live chamber music (🄲 16.00–20.30 Fri & Sat).
🄰 1000 Fifth Avenue 🄣 212 535 7710 🅦 www.metmuseum.org
🄲 09.30–17.30 Tues–Thur & Sun, 09.30–21.00 Fri & Sat, closed Mon
🄼 Subway: 4, 5, 6 to 86th Street

Museum of the City of New York

New York's history from the time the Dutch settled Nieuw
Amsterdam to the present day are located in another of Fifth
Avenue's huge mansions. The 1930 Georgian building houses period
rooms, paintings, sculpture, old photographs and a toy collection.
ⓐ 1220 Fifth Avenue ⓣ 212 534 1672 ⓦ www.mcny.org ⓛ 10.00–17.00
Tues–Sun, 10.00–12.00 Sun (free), closed Mon ⓝ Subway: 6 to 103rd
Street, 2, 3 to Central Park North–110th Street

🔺 *The magnificent interior of the Metropolitan Museum of Art*

Solomon R. Guggenheim Museum

Frank Lloyd Wright is the first artist you meet as you gaze upon his curvaceous building that sits on Fifth Avenue at 89th Street. Wright felt that New York was 'overbuilt, overpopulated, and lacked architectural merit'. Despite his disenchantment, and even his death before its completion, the controversial structure is a monument to Wright's boundless talent, and an icon of 20th-century modernist architecture for the city. Under a soaring glass dome, a continuous ramp slopes gently downwards passing the various collections of Solomon R. Guggenheim. Ongoing exhibits include works of prominent artists: Klee, Picasso, Chagall and Kandinsky. Photography is seen through the eyes of Robert Mapplethorpe. The collection includes art styles from Pollack's abstracts to impressionists Matisse and van Gogh.

🅐 1071 Fifth Avenue 🅣 212 423 3500 🅦 www.guggenheim.org
🅛 10.00–17.45 Sat–Wed, 10.00–19.45 Fri, closed Thur 🅝 Subway: 4, 5, 6 to 86th Street

RETAIL THERAPY

Madison Avenue shopping means high prices for high cheekbones. Home to the likes of Armani and Prada, or Krizia (where a pair of bed sheets costs well over $1,000/£530), only a few 'reasonable' and old-guard shops are tucked in for good measure. Head further east to Lexington Avenue for less pricey places.

Bloomingdales Bloomie's is the adored art deco department store of the east side, and it has never lost its panache. It's well worth browsing, as long as you don't press the button to the 7th floor in the elevator, or you'll end up in designer digs. There are plenty of

mid-priced items elsewhere, and a broad selection of menswear.
🅐 1000 Third Avenue 🕐 212 705 2000 🕐 10.00–20.30 Mon–Fri, until
19.00 Sat, 11.00–19.00 Sun Ⓜ Subway: 4, 5, 6 to 59th Street, N, R, W to
Lexington Avenue–59th Street

The Corner Bookstore As much bookworms as canine lovers, this
tiny shop's staff are known for their friendliness. Alongside its travel,
classics, and children's books, is a neighbourly bulletin board
advising where to find dog-walkers or learn a foreign language.
🅐 1313 Madison Avenue 🕐 212 831 3554 🕐 10.00–20.00 Mon–Thur,
until 19.00 Fri, 11.00–18.00 Sat & Sun Ⓜ Subway: 6 at 96th Street

TAKING A BREAK

In this area of town, you could pay six bucks for a burger, the same
for a cup of coffee, or equip yourself with the best rye bread in the
city and picnic alongside the East River at Carl Schurz Park. Yorkville
was once an enclave of Germans and Hungarians, but few vestiges
of those days have lingered. Gracie Mansion is way over to the East,
too – there's a free Wednesday tour of the official Mayor's home.

Orwasher's Bakery £ ❶ Third-generation bakers make rye
and pumpernickel bread the old-fashioned way, by hand, baked
in a brick-hearth oven. 🅐 308 E 78th Street 🕐 212 288 6569
Ⓦ www.orwashersbakery.com 🕐 07.00–19.00 Mon–Sat,
09.00–16.00 Sun Ⓜ Subway: 4, 5, 6 to 77th Street

Soup Burg £ ❷ Almost old enough to collect social security
payments, this coffee shop burger boutique is low on décor with
its vinyl-topped stools and formica counters. It comes highly

recommended by neighbourhood locals, and is one of those few Madison Avenue addresses with economic prices. ⓐ 922 Madison Avenue ① 212 734 6964 ⓵ 06.00–23.00 Mon–Sun ⓝ Subway: 4, 5, 6 to 77th Street

Café Sabarsky (Neue Galerie) ££ ❸ The jewel-box Neue Galerie, devoted to early 20th-century German and Austrian art, is housed in the elegant townhouse once occupied by Grace Vanderbilt. Even if you can't spend a day seeing the art treasures, get your just desserts at Café Sabarsky. This authentic café serves imported Viennese coffee piled high with schlag (whipped cream), accompanied by pastries to rival any served in Vienna. Try the apple strudel, or the Klimt torte, a hazelnut cake layered with bittersweet chocolate. It's pricey here, but cheaper than a ticket to Austria! ⓐ 1048 Fifth Avenue ① 212 288 0665 ⓦ www.neuegalerie.org ⓵ 11.00–18.00 Sat–Mon, until 21.00 Fri, closed Tues–Thur ⓝ Subway: 4, 5, 6 to 86th Street

⬤ *No escape from the steel architectural add-ons*

AFTER DARK

The best places to go on the Upper East Side are those that the locals frequent. Many are casual, and have aged nicely as their upper-crust clientele returns again and again.

Restaurants
The Carlyle ££ ❹ The Carlyle Hotel is alive with music. Stop by **Bemelmans Bar** for its relaxed atmosphere and drinks, and enjoy whimsical murals by satirist Ludwig Bemelman, creator of the *Madeleine* book series. If you're in for an evening of intimate cabaret, the **Café Carlyle** hosts a variety of entertainers including Woody Allen with his New Orleans jazz band. Entertainment programmes vary in both the bar and café. ⓐ 35 E 76th Street ⓘ 212 744 1600 www.thecarlyle.com ⓛ **Bemelmans** 11.00–01.00 Mon, until 24.00 Sun ⓛ **Café Carlyle** 18.30–24.00, closed Sun ⓝ Subway: 6 to 77th Street

Via Quadronno ££ ❺ Trendy panini bar with Milan-style sandwiches, salads, and more filling entrées at dinner time, with good wines and great espresso. ⓐ 25 E 73rd Street ⓘ 212 650 9880 ⓛ 08.00–23.00 Mon–Fri, 09.00–23.00 Sat, 10.00–21.00 Sun ⓝ Subway: 6 at 77th Street

Elaine's £££ ❻ *She* is an institution now, New York's favourite hostess. It started with her literary friends, and soon the world's celebs were hanging out in this unassuming place. Oh, yes, there's food. ⓐ 1703 Second Avenue ⓘ 212 534 8103 ⓛ 18.00–02.00 Mon–Sat, 17.00–01.00 Sun ⓝ Subway: 4, 5, 6 to 86th Street

Upper West Side

The Upper West Side starts at Columbus Circle and 59th Street. It runs all along Central Park to 110th Street, just below Columbia University, and crosses to West End Avenue and Riverside Drive, overlooking the Hudson River.

Shaped like a pointing finger, at its long northern tip Manhattan narrows dramatically, and is filled with greenscapes, and stunning views. From here, the George Washington Bridge spans the Hudson, and elegantly sparkles at dusk like a diamond necklace. There's a burgeoning interest, these days, in the more northerly neighbourhoods such as Harlem and Washington Heights. The Upper West Side is filled with churches and important museums; trendy spots are popping up everywhere.

SIGHTS & ATTRACTIONS

Elegant art deco and beaux arts buildings line Central Park West. The Dakota, noteworthy as the first large apartment house there, and for its famous couple, Yoko Ono and John Lennon, was built by Henry J Hardenbergh, who also built The Plaza Hotel. Known as an intellectual and artistic neighbourhood, with tree-lined streets and classic brownstones, the Upper West Side is home to several museums and the phenomenal Lincoln Center complex.

It is down the beautiful Central Park West avenue that the world-famous giant balloons float some four storeys tall on their way to Macy's department store each Thanksgiving Day. (If you go, arrive early and dress warmly.)

The Cloisters ↑

WEST 111TH ST

CATHEDRAL PARKWAY

Cathedral
Parkway

Apollo Theater/
Harlem/
Studio Museum

Upper West Side

0   500 metres
0   500 yards

Nicholas
Roerich
Museum

Cathedral of
St John
the Divine

Cathedral
Parkway

WEST 109TH STREET

MANHATTAN
VALLEY

WEST 108TH STREET

WEST 107TH STREET

WEST 106TH STREET

143rd St

WEST 105TH STREET

WEST 104TH STREET

103rd St

Lasker Rink
& Pool

Harlem
Meer

Museum
of the City of
New York

The Loch

WEST 102ND STREET

W 101ST ST

Conservatory
Gardens

The
Pool

Central Park

WEST 100TH STREET

WEST 99TH STREET

**CENTRAL
PARK**

WEST 98TH STREET

WEST 97TH STREET

96th St

North Meadow

TRANSVERSE ROAD NO 4

E 97TH STREET

WEST 96TH ST

WEST 95TH STREET

WEST 94TH STREET

E 95TH STREET

WEST 93RD STREET

E 94TH STREET

WEST 92ND STREET

WEST 91ST STREET

**UPPER
WEST
SIDE**

Jewish
Museum

E 92ND ST

HENRY J BROWNE BOULEVARD (W 90TH ST)

Croton
Reservoir

Cooper-Hewitt National
Design Museum

WEST 89TH STREET

**CARNEGIE
HILL**

WEST 88TH STREET

WEST 87TH STREET

Solomon R. Guggenheim
Museum

Soldiers and
Sailors Monument

WEST 86TH STREET

86th St

WEST 85TH STREET

86th St

E 86TH STREET

EDGAR ALLAN POE ST (W 84TH ST) ❶

WEST 83RD ST

**The Great
Lawn**

TRANSVERSE   ROAD   NO 3

Children's Museum
of Manhattan

WEST 82ND STREET

Hudson River

81st St -
Museum of
Natural History

Cleopatra's
Needle

Metropolitan
Museum
of Art

E 85TH STREET

WEST 81ST STREET

Hayden
Planetarium

WEST 80TH STREET

79th St

Delacorte
Theater

Goethe-Institut

WEST 78TH STREET

WEST 77TH STREET

❻

American
Museum
of Natural
History

Belvedere
Castle

Turtle
Pond

E 80TH STREET

E 79TH STREET

TRANSVERSE   ROAD   NO 2

E 78TH STREET

WEST 76TH STREET

The Ramble

WEST 75TH STREET

Statue of Alice
in Wonderland

E 77TH STREET

WEST 74TH STREET

WEST 73RD STREET

The
Lake

Loeb
Boathouse

Harkness
House

72nd St

WEST 72ND STREET

72nd St

Statue of
Hans Christian
Andersen

Whitney Museum
of American Art

❷

WEST 71ST STREET

Strawberry
Fields

Bethesda
Fountain

EAST 72ND STREET

WEST 70TH STREET

EAST 71ST STREET

WEST 69TH STREET

Lincoln
Towers

WEST 68TH STREET

WEST 67TH STREET

**Central
Park**

The Frick
Collection

EAST 70TH STREET

E 69TH STREET

Alice Tully Hall

W 66TH ST

Museum of
American
Folk Art

❸

The Sheep
Meadow

Center for
African Art

E 68TH STREET

**LENOX
HILL**

WEST 66TH STREET

WEST 65TH STREET

TRANSVERSE   ROAD   NO 1

E 66TH STREET

Lincoln Center for
the Performing Arts

The Dairy
Visitor Center

S. D. Roosevelt
Memorial House

**LINCOLN
CENTER**

W 64TH ST

W 63RD ST

Fordham
University

Wollman
Memorial Rink

Wildlife
Center

W 62ND ST

W 61ST ST

Heckscher
Playground

W 60TH ST

New York
Coliseum

The Pond

W 59TH ST

59th St -
Columbus
Circle

Maine
Memorial

COLUMBUS

WEST SIDE HIGHWAY (MILLER HIGHWAY)

FREEDOM PLACE

WEST END AVENUE

AMSTERDAM AVENUE

BROADWAY

COLUMBUS AVENUE

CENTRAL PARK WEST

FIFTH AVENUE

MADISON AVENUE

LENOX AVENUE

RIVERSIDE DRIVE

9A

HENRY HUDSON PARKWAY

CATHEDRAL
PARKWAY

M .....Metro Stop
✝ .....Cathedral
ℹ .....Information
✈ .....Airport
🚆 .....Railway Stn
✚ .....Hospital
⚫ .....Police

N

THE CITY

Cathedral of St John the Divine

Still the world's largest gothic cathedral, and still under construction, this is as much a religious centre as a museum and cultural centre, with a modern attitude. Stained-glass windows depict sports, American history, and medicine, as well as religious subjects. Carved statues of saints adorn the High Altar, but there are also likenesses of Christopher Columbus and Abraham Lincoln. Then there's the live elephant in the processional on St Francis Day. Located in Morningside Heights, near Columbia University.

Behold the beautiful skyline of Manhattan

1047 Amsterdam Avenue 212 316 7540 www.stjohndivine.org
07.00–18.00 Mon–Sat, 07.00–19.00 Sun Subway: 1, 9 to 110th Street–Cathedral Parkway Station

Columbus Circle

New York's only roundabout, a kind of revolving door between midtown and New York's cultural epicentre, is a tangle of traffic surrounded by multi-storey skyscrapers. Located at the corner of Central Park West on W 59th Street, Huntington Hartford's art museum is one of the few low-rise buildings left, and will be reincarnated as the American Craft Museum. The Donald's (Trump,

of course) Hotel towers over the circle, but it's the all-glass, glitzy, new Time-Warner Center that's in the news. Its mall, more politely known as 'The Shops', brings 40 brand-name stores, and top designers to the neighbourhood, with Cartier, Williams-Sonoma and Thomas Pink among them. Trendy but pricey restaurants like Per Se and Masa top the list of numerous eateries.

Steps away is the Mandarin Oriental Hotel – it's worth stopping for cocktails at its lofty Mobar for the view. Come here mid-morning on Sunday, when traffic is non-existent, and enjoy the beauty of the circle and its statue of Columbus. Skip the glass giants, and walk up Central Park West for brunch at pricey Tavern on the Green, or breakfast at not-so-pricey Good Enough to Eat.

Harlem

When southern Black people migrated north, Harlem was their destination. They brought vitality to the area, especially during the Harlem Renaissance, a golden era of literature and the arts (1919–29). It was a time when the city became known as 'The Big Apple'; the place was rocking and the sound of jazz flowed through the air. Black Americans brought their religion and built many churches, they brought their soul food (nearly a religion), and established a bustling society.

Stroll through the area and wonder at the mix of grandiose brownstones and dingy tenements. Places to see include lovely row houses in Hamilton Heights (also known as Sugar Hill), once home to Chief Justice Thurgood Marshall, and Sugar Ray Robinson. Striver's Row has elegant Sanford White-designed town homes – the word on the street is 'Move over SoHo, here comes Harlem'.

Hunt for bargains at the Malcolm Shabazz market, stop on 125th Street at Malcolm X Corner, but don't miss the Studio Museum (w www.studiomuseum.org), the Apollo Theater, or a gospel service at the Abyssinian Baptist Church on W 138th Street.

CULTURE

The cultural opportunities on the Upper West Side have wide appeal. The Natural History exhibits and Planetarium are especially popular with both adults and children.

American Museum of Natural History

Every true New Yorker has spent time on the learning curve in this sprawling museum covering everything in creation. Dinosaur delirium is alive and well in the vaulted Rotunda, where a barosaurus skeleton stands 152 m (50 ft) high on its hind legs. More dinosaurs and pterodactyls with scientific names too long to remember occupy three large halls in the museum.

Highlights include dioramas that trace Asian, African and South American peoples, and others depicting frozen-in-time animal life. The Hall of Ocean Life exhibits a 28.5 m (94 ft) blue whale. There's a 34 ton meteorite, and Santiago Calatrava's stainless steel *Times Capsule*. In the new, ultra-modern Rose Center for Earth and Space, you can see the Planetarium sphere, and the new *Cosmic Collisions* space show. Here, too, is an IMAX theatre. On the first Friday of every month, *Starry Nights* features live jazz, while you sip Sangria and nibble tapas in the Rose Center (ⓒ Until 20.45).

ⓐ 79th Street at Central Park ⓣ 212 769 5200 ⓦ www.amnh.org
ⓒ 10.00–17.45 Mon–Sun ⓢ Subway: B, C to 81st Street

Apollo Theater

The legendary Apollo Theater helped to put black music into America's mainstream. Among those discovered at the Apollo are music greats such as Ella Fitzgerald, Aretha Franklin and Count Basie. Wednesday's Amateur Night, which showcases young talent in competition, is a hoot.

ⓐ 253 W 125th Street ⓣ 212 531 5300 ⓦ www.apollotheater.com
ⓝ Subway: 1, 9 to 125th Street

The Cloisters

Step back into medieval times with a visit to the Cloisters, high on a hill over the Hudson River. The collection features art and architecture from the Middle Ages (part of the Metropolitan Museum of Art). Stained glass, enamels, icons and the famous Belgian Unicorn tapestries are on exhibit. The exquisite Cuxa Cloister (12th century), with its pink marble columns from a French abbey, surrounds a square flower garden.

ⓐ Fort Tryon Park ⓣ 212 923 3700 ⓦ www.metmuseum.org
ⓛ 09.30–16.45 Tues–Sun, closed Mon (Nov–end Feb); 09.30–17.15 Tues–Sun, closed Mon (Mar–end Oct) ⓝ Subway: A to 190th Street; Bus: M4 to the Cloisters

Lincoln Center for the Performing Arts

In its relatively short life, Lincoln Center has grown to include everything from the 'a' in aria to the 'z' in jazz. In one central place, it includes the acoustically unsurpassed Alice Tully Hall (chamber music), the Avery Fisher Hall, the Metropolitan Opera House, the New York City Ballet, the New York City Opera, the New York Philharmonic Orchestra, the New York State Theater, the Vivian Beaumont Theater, the Walter Reade Theater for the centre's film society, the Julliard School of Music, a Library and a Museum. In winter, the Big Apple Circus pitches its tents on the centre's huge plaza. Best of all, when summer comes, the Plaza is transformed into a swinging spot full of music, where New Yorkers and visitors come to dance the night away. Ⓐ 70 Lincoln Center Plaza (Broadway at W 64th Street) ❶ 212 875 5456 Ⓦ www.lincolncenter.org Ⓝ Subway: 1, 9 to 66th Street

🔺 *Imagine: the talent the world can't forget*

Strawberry Fields, Central Park

The Beatles' song 'Strawberry Fields Forever' inspired this garden of peace to honour John Lennon, who died a tragic death at the hands of a fanatic fan. The tear-shaped park, chosen by John's wife, Yoko Ono, was one of Lennon's favourite spots. A simple mosaic, based on one from Pompeii, bears the single word, *IMAGINE*, the title of another Lennon song. Visitors walk under shady trees along curving paths, and pay their respects.

ⓐ Central Park – W 71st to 74th Streets ⓦ www.centralparknyc.org

TAKING A BREAK

You can get some fresh air over near the Hudson River at the 79th Street Boat Basin. Or stop at one of the area's famous delis – Zabar's, for one, at 80th Street and Broadway.

Good Enough to Eat £ ❶ This all-American comfort-food eatery offers a feast on a healthy platter of pancakes, bacon and eggs, or try the speciality pumpkin bread toast ⓐ 483 Amsterdam Avenue ⓣ 212 496 0163 ⓦ www.goodenoughtoeat.com ⓛ 08.00–22.30 Mon–Thur, 09.00–23.00 Fri–Sat, 09.00–22.00 Sun ⓝ Subway: 1 to 79th Street, B, C to 81st Street

Gray's Papaya £ ❷ The greatest 75¢ hot dog in town – wash it down with papaya juice ⓐ 2090 Broadway ⓣ 212 799 0243 ⓛ 24 hours a day ⓝ Subway: 1, B, C to 72nd Street

Tavern on the Green ££–£££ ❸ Stop at the Tavern for Sunday brunch, and enjoy the view and outdoor garden. ⓐ W 67th Street and Central Park West ⓣ 212 873 3200

Ⓦ www.tavernonthegreen.com Ⓛ 11.30–15.00 Mon–Fri, 17.00–22.00
Sun–Thur, 10.00–15.00 Sat & Sun, 17.00–22.30 Fri & Sat Ⓝ Subway:
1 to 66th Street

AFTER DARK

Most restaurants around Lincoln Center offer an early start for
dinner, giving customers plenty of time to make curtain call. There
are restaurants offering food from a huge variety of international
cuisines – and, of course, soul food – in Harlem.

Restaurants

Awash £ ❹ Casual Ethiopian – tasty gomen besiga: sautéed
beef, collard greens, onions and just a bit of cardamon.
Ⓐ 947 Amsterdam Avenue Ⓣ 212 961 1416 Ⓦ www.awashnyc.com
Ⓛ 13.00–24.00 Mon–Fri, 12.00–24.00 Sat & Sun Ⓝ Subway: 1, 9 to
103rd Street

Sylvia's £ ❺ Finger-lickin' soul food at its best. Be sure to try
the Queen's collard greens, tender ribs, and candied yams. Ⓐ 328
Lenox Avenue Ⓣ 212 996 0660 Ⓦ www.sylviassoulfood.com
Ⓛ 08.00–22.30 Mon–Sat, 11.00–20.00 Sun Ⓝ Subway: 2, 3 to
125th Street

En Plo ££ ❻ Enjoy fresh whole grilled fish with lemon and
capers in this Greek countryside-style restaurant. Downstairs
in the Ouzerie, live music or a DJ will have you dancing on the
tables. Ⓐ 103 W 77th Street Ⓣ 212 579 7777 Ⓦ www.enplonyc.com
Ⓛ 12.00–23.00 Mon–Thur, 12.00–24.00 Fri & Sat; Music 10.00–04.00
Thur–Sat Ⓝ Subway: C, 1, 2, 3 to 72nd Street

Greenwich Village

In the 1820s, wealthy downtowners fled to the Village, escaping a bustling, bawdy metropolis. When the Village grew, they fled further uptown. A century or so later, counter-culture uptowners reversed gears. Bohemians, free-thinkers, artists and poets came downtown to the quiet charm of this now historical area.

For many years, Greenwich Village differentiated between the East Village and the West Village. Nowadays that division is fuzzy, but one thing's for sure, Greenwich Village starts at Washington Arch and around sprawling New York University. Fortunately, as a historical landmark district, the Village is protected. People come to wander – slipping into cosy restaurants, and hunting for little treasures, like sifting sand for specks of gold. As dusk settles in, they look for good theatre and the thrill of techno until dawn.

SIGHTS & ATTRACTIONS

It's both easy and delightful to get lost along the lovely, tree-lined streets that wind, without rhyme or reason, through the fabric of the Village. It's a place that twists and turns – where West 10th crosses West 4th, and Waverly crosses Waverly (yes, it's a fact!).

Architecture, artists and authors

In a swampy wasteland far north of Wall Street there was a gallows at the Hanging Elm in the 1800s. The spot had been a paupers' burial ground, and duelling ground. It was incomprehensible at the time that this square would eventually be surrounded by elegant 19th-century townhouses. **A Triumphal Arch** designed by Stanford White (modelled after Paris' Arc de Triomphe) was erected there to

mark the centenary of George Washington's inauguration. It marks the downtown end of Fifth Avenue, and the beginning of street confusion. One snowy eve in 1917, the Arch was the scene of a raucous party when six revellers climbed atop to declare Greenwich Village 'a free and independent republic'.

Washington Square Park has its share of literary and artistic history. Edward Hopper lived at No 3, one of the remaining Greek Revival row houses. Henry James visited his grandmother there, subsequently naming a novel, *Washington Square*. The park shed its druggy days, replaced now, by impromptu musicians, a few chess hustlers and skateboarders. An art show takes place here in spring and autumn, under the watchful eye of the ageing Hanging Elm.

Gertrude Vanderbilt Whitney worked as a sculptor on **MacDougal Alley** (the converted stables). She amassed artworks of friends, and established her own museum on W 8th Street after the Met snubbed their nose at her gift offer for the collection. (She later established the **Whitney Museum of American Art**.)

C.O. Bigelow is around the corner on Sixth Avenue. It has the distinction of being the oldest apothecary in the US, open since 1838. During the 1977 blackout, they simply lit their working gas lamps, and it was business as usual.

A turreted, 1876 Victorian-Gothic structure, **Jefferson Market Courthouse**, looks completely out of place on busy Sixth Avenue, and is now a public library. Surrounding one-time bordellos are now gift shops, cafés and a hairdresser. An elevated train ran along the avenue, then known as Lady's Mile. **Patchin Place** is easy to miss; the

⏵ *Beautiful stained glass is a feature of Greenwich's Church of the Ascension*

small cul de sac with ten Federal townhouses was home to Theodore Dreiser, author of *An American Tragedy*, e e Cummings, and O'Henry.

Around the corner on W 11th Street is the tiny, triangular cemetery of the Spanish and Portuguese Synagogue; only a few headstones remain. Further up the street, a Greek Revival house was destroyed when a bomb made by the Weathermen accidentally exploded; neighbour Dustin Hoffman escaped unharmed.

At the corner of W 10th Street on Fifth Avenue is the Richard Upjohn-designed, **Church of the Ascension**. Stanford White commissioned Louis Comfort Tiffany and John LaFarge stained-glass windows for the church.

Federal style, 77 Bedford Street is the oldest house in the Village. Next door is New York's narrowest house, which measures less than 3 m (10 ft) in width.

Louisa May Alcott wrote *Little Women* while living at Nos 130–132 MacDougal, and the Provincetown Playhouse premiered many of Eugene O'Neill's plays, who lived at No. 133.

The east side of the Village also has architectural treasures, many associated with the John Jacob Astor Family. On Lafayette Street is Colonnade Row (No. 428), once occupied by Astors and Vanderbilts, and the Puck Building (No. 295) with its charming statue, which housed the German-language magazine *Puck*. The **Public Theater** was originally the Astor Library (No. 425).

CULTURE

In contrast to the city's huge, uptown museums, the Village is full of art galleries and small collections. But don't be fooled; the quality here is unrivalled.

Forbes Magazine Galleries

The passion of magazine magnate, Malcolm Forbes, is the basis for the idiosyncratic collection in this petite museum. Among the exhibits are 10,000 marching toy soldiers in battle, presidential papers, Abraham Lincoln's stovepipe hat, and early versions of the Monopoly® game. An exhibition of jewellery collections of famous persons includes the Scorpio Pendant that belonged to Princess Grace.

📍 62 Fifth Avenue ☎ 212 206 5548 🕐 10.00–16.00 Tues, Wed, Fri & Sat, closed Sun, Mon & Thur Ⓝ Subway: R, W to 8th Street, F, V to 14th Street

Merchant's House Museum

By virtue of remaining in one family, the Federalist house built for Seabury Tredwell in 1832 is New York's only home preserved intact – inside and out. Left to the city by the wealthy merchant's eighth child, it contains many of the family's original furniture, memorabilia, their period clothing, and even needlework and family photographs.

📍 29 E 4th Street ☎ 212 777 1089 Ⓦ www.merchantshouse.com 🕐 12.00–17.00 Thur–Mon, closed Tues & Wed Ⓝ Subway: N or R to 8th Street, 6 to Astor Place, F, B to Broadway–Lafayette

RETAIL THERAPY

Thanks to low-rise architecture, the Village is filled with small stores, often with unique and one-of-a-kind items. Some of it is sobering, but more is funky, and the further east the shop, the punkier things get. There are plenty of places for body piercing or tattoos, if that's your pleasure. A permanent street market has taken over 8th Street at Third Avenue, with no real menu of products, but expect good finds in used records. Some designer stores have moved in, especially on the northwestern end of Bleecker Street where the likes of Ralph Lauren and Marc Jacobs have set up shop.

C.O. Bigelow Mark Twain got his prescriptions from this old world apothecary, which sells hand-milled soaps, old-fashioned

⬥ *The Strand Book Store is home to 18 miles of books*

toothpaste, and ancient (but currently trendy) homeopathic remedies. The customer comes first at this 167-year-old store.
ⓐ 414 Sixth Avenue ⓣ 212 533 2700 ⓦ www.bigelowchemists.com
ⓛ 07.30–21.00 Mon–Fri, 08.30–19.00 Sat, 09.00–17.00 Sun
ⓝ Subway: R to 8th Street, F to 14th Street

Marc Jacobs The designer's edgy style in his more affordable line, Marc by Marc, includes collections for both genders.
ⓐ 403 Bleecker Street ⓣ 212 924 0026 ⓦ www.marcjacobs.com
ⓛ 12.00–20.00 Mon–Sat, 12.00–19.00 Sun ⓝ Subway: A, C, E to 14th Street, L to Eighth Avenue

Strand Book Store A treasure chest filled with miles of review and second-hand books sold here at super-bargain prices. Specialities include, collectables, hard-to-find, and rare books. ⓐ 828 Broadway
ⓣ 212 473 1452 ⓦ www.strandbooks.com ⓛ 09.20–22.30 Mon–Sat, 11.00–22.30 Sun ⓝ Subway: L, N, R, 4, 5, 6 to 14th Street–Union Square

TAKING A BREAK

New Yorkers love to people-watch. With all the sidewalk cafés, squares, and parks, it's the perfect place to sit back, don a pair of sunglasses, and watch the fashion show.

Joe Jr. £ ❶ Grab a quick bite in the quintessential family-owned diner, great for burgers and Greek specials – Isaac Mizrahi orders his morning coffee here. Lots of regulars and 'hey-I'm-normal' celebs.
ⓐ 482 Sixth Avenue ⓣ 212 924 5220 ⓛ 06.00–01.00 ⓝ Subway: F, V, L, 1, 2, 3 to 14th Street

Angelica Kitchen £–££ 'Strict veggies for vegans' has a huge following, lots of food and good value. Try the Dragon Bowl with rice, beans, tofu, steamed and sea veggies. 🄰 300 E 12th Street 🄵 212 228 209 🅆 www.angelicakitchen.com 🄻 11.30–22.30 🄽 Subway: F, V to Lower East Side–Second Avenue

White Horse Tavern ££ Another literary relic is the 1880s pub frequented by Dylan Thomas. Refreshing pale ale is served in tall mugs; good bar food, with outdoor seating. 🄰 567 Hudson Street 🄵 212 243 9260 🄻 11.00–02.00 Sun–Thur, 11.00–04.00 Fri & Sat 🄽 Subway: 1 to Christopher Street–Sheridan Square

AFTER DARK

In the West Village, jazz and Off-Broadway theatre share the same haunted streets where cappuccino is king, and ghosts of New York's literary and artistic past live on at cafés and bars. Over on the east side, curry and pirogies (boiled dumplings and sautéed onion with a filling) cohabit with veggies and wraps. Among little enclaves of Ukrainian, Indian and Japanese eateries, stylish restaurants are moving in. Gentrification is a keyword in this area.

🄸 Reminder: many places don't take credit cards!

Restaurants
Momofuku Noodle Bar £ Ramen, Korean buckwheat noodles, and BBQ pork buns are served at a long wooden bar. 🄰 163 First Avenue 🄵 212 475 7899 🄻 12.00–23.00 Sun–Thur, 12.00–24.00 Fri & Sat 🄽 Subway: F, V to Second Avenue, L to First Avenue, 6 to Astor Place

La Nacional £ ❺ An unmarked door leads to unsurpassed paella in this very special Argentinean spot. Featuring Flamenco performances on Fri & Sat, and Tango Thursdays (🕘 Lessons 19.00–21.30; Dancing until 02.00). ⓐ 239 W 14th Street ① 212 243 9308 Ⓦ www.tangolanacional.com 🕘 Dinner: 12.00–23.00 Wed–Sat, 12.00–22.00 Sun–Tues Ⓝ Subway: A, C, E, F, L, V, 1, 2, 3 to 14th Street

Veselka £ ❻ This Ukrainian diner is open around the clock. From breakfast to the après-club scene, expect queues out the door for its pirogies or kielbasa. Borscht or chilled summer soups follow the seasons. ⓐ 144 Second Avenue ① 212 228 9682 Ⓝ Subway: 6 to Astor Place

Yaffa Café £ ❼ The emphasis here is on healthy food and vegetarian dishes in a funky subterranean setting, very much for the after-hours crowd. It has an outdoor garden for summer dining. ⓐ 97 Saint Marks Place ① 212 674 9302 Ⓦ www.yaffacafe.com 🕘 24 hours a day Ⓝ Subway: L to First Avenue, 6 to Astor Place

Japonica ££ ❽ Fresh, high-quality and large portions of sushi are the trademark of this restaurant, popular with local regulars. ⓐ 100 University Place ① 212 243 7752 🕘 12.00–22.30 Mon–Thur, 12.00–23.00 Fri, 13.00–23.00 Sat, 13.00–22.30 Sun Ⓝ Subway: L, N, R, 4, 5, 6 to 14th Street–Union Square

Mary's Fish Camp ££ ❾ A tiny space with titanic hunks of succulence in the super fresh, lightly herbed lobster rolls. ⓐ 64 Charles Street ① 646 486 2185 Ⓦ www.marysfishcamp.com 🕘 12.00–15.00, 18.00–23.00 Mon–Sat, closed Sun Ⓝ Subway: 1, 9 to Christopher Street–Sheridan Square

ON THIS SITE
IN 1897 NOTHING
HAPPENED

Massimo al Ponte Vecchio ££ ⑩ Chef Massimo Rellini brought his Neapolitan accent and family cuisine from Italy. He cooks Zuppa di fagioli (cannellini bean soup with pasta) his mother's way. Tender venison loin with balsamic vinegar sauce melts in the mouth. ⓐ 206 Thompson Street ⓣ 212 228 7701 ⓦ www.massimoalpontevecchio.com ⓛ 12.00–15.00 Mon–Fri, 16.00–23.00 Mon–Sat, 12.00–22.00 Sun ⓝ Subway: A, B, C, D, E, F, Q to W 4th Street–Washington Square

Otto Enoteca ££ ⑪ Tapas, and new-wave pizza, like Mario Batali's lardo pie, are griddle cooked in an Italian train depot atmosphere. There's a younger crowd on weekends in a buzzing bar and restaurant. ⓐ 1 Fifth Avenue ⓣ 212 995 9559 ⓦ www.ottopizzeria.com ⓛ 11.30–24.00 Mon–Sun ⓝ Subway: A, C, E, B, D, F, V to W 4th Street

Spotted Pig ££ ⑫ Trendy a-la-gastro-pub has yummy smoked trout and many Italian dishes. It became so crowded, they opened a second floor. ⓐ 314 W 11th Street ⓣ 212 620 0393 ⓦ www.thespottedpig.com ⓛ 12.00–02.00 Mon–Fri, 11.00–02.00 Sat & Sun ⓝ L to Eighth Avenue, A, C, E to 14th Street, 1 to Christopher Street–Sheridan Square

Il Cantinori £££ ⑬ Northern Tuscan dishes are served in a romantic and relaxed atmosphere. The restaurant is decorated with stunning floral arrangements. It's a low-key favourite with locals and celebs. The magic is in the simplicity of their Petto D'Anatra con Lenticchie (duck breast with lentils). Summer sidewalk patio. ⓐ 32 E 10th Street

◀ *Standing guard outside a place where 'nothing happened'*

212 673 6044 www.ilcantinori.com 12.00–14.30, 17.30–23.30 Mon–Thur, 12.00–14.30, 17.30–24.00 Fri, 17.30–24.00 Sat, 17.30–23.30 Sun Subway: L, N, R, 4, 5, 6 to 14th Street–Union Square

Cinemas & theatres

Joseph Papp Public Theater Half a dozen theatres produce a wide variety of award-winning plays, musicals and Shakespeare at low ticket prices or for free. The Public opened with *Hair*, brought plays like *The Chorus Line* to Broadway, and vows to continue innovative cultural projects. *Film at the Public* offers cutting edge art cinema. 425 Lafayette Street www.publictheater.org Subway: N, R, W to 8th Street, 6 to Astor Place

Bars, clubs & discos

Arthur's Tavern It's been around long enough for the paint to fade, but that's just part of the charm. Monday's Dixieland band is always on the programme. Jazz sets play other nights from 19.00–21.00, then the crowd mellows away the night with blues or R&B. 57 Grove Street 212 675 6879 www.arthurstavernnyc.com 20.00–04.00 Sun–Mon, 18.30–04.00 Tues–Sat Subway: 1 to Christopher Street–Sheridan Square

Bowlmor Can a 42-lane cavernous bowling alley be cutting edge? Monday Night Strike special has glow-in-the-dark bowling to a live DJ beat all night long for $20/£11. It's said that Nixon bowled here. 110 University Place 212 255 8188 www.bowlmor.com 11.00–03.00 Mon, until 01.00 Tues & Wed, until 02.00 Thur, until 04.00 Fri & Sat, until 24.00 Sun Subway: L, N, Q, R, W, 4, 5, 6 to 14th Street–Union Square

Chumley's Still no sign outside, it was a Prohibition speakeasy. Sit next to the fireplace and reminisce about your favourite authors over a good beer and bar food. F Scott Fitzgerald, John Steinbeck and John Dos Passos took refuge here. 🄰 86 Bedford Street 🄣 212 675 4449 🄛 16.00–23.00 Mon–Thur, until 02.00 Fri, 10.00–02.00 Sat, 13.00–02.00 Sun 🄽 Subway: 1, 9 to Christopher Street

Decibel Sake away in a graffiti-cluttered basement, but don't fret if it's hard to choose from the 60 brands of rice wine. Shrimp and seaweed tidbits at the bar. 🄰 240 E 9th Street 🄣 212 929 2733 🄛 20.00–02.50 Mon–Sat, 20.00–00.50 Sun 🄽 Subway: 6 to Astor Place

Hudson Bar & Books A serious whiskey bar with light fare and a twist – smoking is allowed! Cigars, wine and mixed drinks are served in an elegant library. Other perks include James Bond 007 movies, and free internet access (🄛 17.00–20.00). 🄰 636 Hudson Street 🄣 212 229 2642 🄦 www.barandbooks.cz 🄛 16.30–02.00 Mon–Fri, 18.00–04.00 Sat & Sun 🄽 Subway: A, C, E, L to 14th Street

Joe's Pub An intimate cabaret venue that showcases live music and emerging artists, ranging from international rock bands through the underground pop scene to East Village entertainers, or old pros like Eartha Kitt. Dinner also served. 🄰 425 Lafayette Street 🄦 www.joespub.com 🄛 Dinner: 18.00–22.30 🄽 Subway: N, R, W to 8th Street, 6 to Astor Place

Eclectic neighbourhoods

The soul of New York lies in its neighbourhoods, and in recent history some forgotten areas have catapulted into the limelight. Over hundreds of years, ethnic groups gave New York character, integrating their culture wherever they lived and worked. Ethnicity and cultural mix is at its most diverse in the Lower East Side, Chinatown and Little Italy. Many areas have been revitalised recently. Artists looked for large spaces in which to work. New inhabitants brought their own creativity and personality, which permeated areas such as Chelsea, Union Square, SoHo and Tribeca (Triangle Below Canal). The latest neighbourhood to receive a facelift is the Meatpacking District. Who could imagine that a bunch of shack-like warehouses, designed for meat hooks, would appear consummately attractive to hot designers, celebs like Julia Roberts, and trend-setting chefs? But, *voilà*, the blue collar is gone and avant-garde has moved in.

SIGHTS & ATTRACTIONS

You have to walk these neighbourhoods to absorb their subtle and not-so-subtle differences – Gramercy Park with its genteel nature; SoHo and Tribeca with their beautiful old cast-iron buildings and vibrant lifestyle; the Lower East Side with its mix of old with new; and Chelsea and the Meatpacking District (between Chelsea and the West Village), the home of cutting-edge galleries and hip boutiques.

Eldridge Street Synagogue

One of the few survivors of nearly 500 Lower East Side synagogues is this famous one on Eldridge Street, currently under restoration. Its

Eclectic neighbourhoods

0   500 metres
0   500 yards

MIDTOWN SOUTH

CHELSEA

Joyce Theater

Rubin Museum of Art

FLAT IRON

Fire Boat Station

WEST VILLAGE

GREENWICH VILLAGE

Hudson River

Flatiron Building

Th. Roosevelt Birthplace

N.Y. Police Museum

Forbes Magazine Galleries

Cons. Edison Energy Mus.

Washington Square Park

GREENWICH VILLAGE

SOHO

New Museum of Contemporary Art

LITTLE ITALY

TRIBECA

CHINA TOWN

Tenement Museum

Eldridge Street Synagogue

LOWER EAST SIDE

Hamilton Fish Park

Seward Park

Columbus Park

Vladeck Park

Wallabout Bay

	Metro Stop
	Cathedral
	Information
	Airport
	Railway Stn
	Hospital
	Police

façade and interior mix Gothic stained-glass windows with Moorish arches. A beautiful walnut ark is intricately hand-carved, and *trompe l'oeil* murals fill the walls, under high vaulted ceilings. Among its worshippers were Dr Jonas Salk, inventor of the polio vaccine, and actor Edward G Robinson.

ⓐ 12 Eldridge Street ⓦ www.eldridgestreet.org ⓣ 212 219 0903 ⓛ 11.00–16.00 Tues–Thur & Sun, closed Mon, Fri & Sat ⓝ Subway: F to E Broadway, B, D to Grand Street, N, R, 6 to Canal Street

Flatiron Building

This unusual 22-storey triangular building, reputed to be the city's first skyscraper, is New York's sweetheart landmark. Some say it resembles the bow of an ocean liner, or a flat iron (its adopted nickname). It appears as the offices of *The Daily Bugle* in the *Spiderman* movies.

ⓐ 175 Fifth Avenue at Broadway ⓝ Subway: B, D, R, 1, 6 to 23rd Street

Little Italy

The aroma of bakeries and pasta fills the air on Mulberry Street, where the Feast of San Gennaro takes place in September.

ⓦ www.littleitalynyc.com ⓝ Subway: F, V to Broadway–Lafayette, N, R to Prince Street, 6 to Spring Street

Lower East Side

This was the gateway to America some 200 years ago. Newcomers squeezed into dismal, teeming tenements around Orchard Street. Streets were clogged with throngs of people and pushcarts piled high with potatoes, and it was a bustling

◀ *The Eldridge Street synagogue is an awe-inspiring building*

commercial centre, before becoming an historic Jewish area, and then a Latino neighbourhood. As fortunes changed, Latinos moved in but, until recently, few New Yorkers frequented the derelict area. The tenements are still there, but the old, abysmal apartments are now duplex haunts of today's hipsters and dot.comers. Where the language on the street was Yiddish, it's now the stylish lingo of people on the move – downtown – the reverse direction their ancestors took when they escaped uptown. Many shops are closed Saturday and open Sunday.

 Subway: J, M, Z to Essex Street, F to Delancey Street

SoHo cast-iron buildings

Coined for its location south of Houston Street (pronounced how-stun), SoHo is home to a historic district filled with late 1800s cast-iron buildings. The king of Greene Street (Nos 72–76) is considered the finest of 50 elaborately decorated buildings along five cobblestone blocks. Nearby, is the art nouveau queen of Greene Street (Nos 28–30). Two more architecturally notable buildings are on Broadway. The Little Singer Building (yes, it's named after the sewing machine), a beaux arts beauty at Nos 561–563, is an ornate terracotta structure adorned with wrought-iron balconies and dark green arches. The other is the Haughwout Building at Nos 488–491, with rows of arch-framed windows set on columns. Now the neighbourhood is filled with artists' lofts and art galleries.

 Subway: A, C, E, J, N, Q, R, 6 to Canal Street

CULTURE

One might easily say that downtown is immersed in art and culture. Slip into the landmark Chelsea Hotel, and see its art-filled lobby. Emerging Tribeca artists hold a springtime event called TOAST (Tribeca Open Artist Studio Tour), when locals open their basements, lofts and even rooftops to share their work with the public (www.toastartwalk.com). SoHo is laughing with its Museum of Comic and Cartoon Art (www.moccany.org), and there's something for everyone, even for hedonists; check out Chelsea's Museum of Sex (www.museumofsex.com).

Galleries

Chelsea, SoHo, and now Meatpacking, have a hefty share of the city's art galleries. The Meatpacking District has Wooster Projects with David Hockney and Andy Warhol pieces, and Chelsea has Sonnabend, the Paula Cooper Gallery, and Gagosian. SoHo started the whole gallery thing, and its Museum Row on Broadway includes a downtown version of the Guggenheim, and Whitney's offshoot, the New Museum of Contemporary Art. The Museum for African Art is located in the same building.

Rubin Museum of Art

Truly unique, this museum is dedicated to Himalayan art.
📍 150 W 17th Street 📞 212 620 5000 🌐 www.rmanyc.org
🕐 11.00–17.00 Mon & Thur, 11.00–19.00 Wed, 11.00–22.00 Fri, 11.00–18.00 Sat & Sun, closed Tues 🚇 Subway: 1 to 18th Street, A, C, E to Eighth Avenue, F to 14th Street

Tenement Museum

The experience of sweatshop garment workers and immigrants crammed into tiny quarters is relived in this preserved museum in an 1863 tenement house. The very popular interpretive tours visit different period apartments.

Museum Center 108 Orchard Street 212 431 8420
 www.tenement.org
1863 House Tours 212 431 0233 13.00–16.30 Tues–Fri, 10.00–17.00
Sat & Sun (no tours Mon) Subway: F to Delancey, B, D to Grand
Street, J, M, Z to Essex Street.

RETAIL THERAPY

Shopping is an eclectic feast in these neighbourhoods, and the
choices range from splashing out on your credit card to happy
haggling. In its mere 0.6 sq km (0.25 sq mile), SoHo has its edgy haute
couture and fun clothing, not to mention the famous art supply
stores (Compleat Sculptor and Pearl Paint). Further south in Tribeca
and NoLita (North of Little Italy), gorgeous goodies include one-of-a-
kind treasures found on Mulberry and Mott Streets. The Lower East
Side has its share of boutiques, too, but you'll definitely want to seek
out bargains in discount shops. Bargains can be had in Chelsea at
Loehmann's, but it's more of a chic boutique neighbourhood. Top
designers are fast and furious in the Meatpacking District, but don't
trip over a sidewalk vault-cover in your fancy new Jeffrey shoes.

Diane von Furstenberg Her slinky, soft little wraps have been
newsmakers for two decades. 385 W 12th Street 646 486 4800
 www.dvf.com 11.00–18.00 Mon & Fri, 11.00–19.00 Tues & Wed,
11.00–20.00 Thur, 11.00–17.00 Sat, 12.00–17.00 Sun Subway: A, C, E
to 14th Street, L to Eighth Avenue Meatpacking

 Classic architecture of the Bowery Street area

Fragments An emporium showcasing 25 up-and-coming jewellery designers. 116 Prince Street 212 334 9588
www.fragments.com 10.00–18.00 Mon–Sat, 12.00–17.00 Sun
Subway: N, R to Prince Street

Issey Miyake Sleek, shiny, silky, wearable art is worth a look in this high-tech Tribeca shop. 119 Hudson Street 212 226 0100
www.isseymiyake.com 11.00–19.00 Mon–Sat, 12.00–18.00 Sun
Subway: 1 to Franklin Street

Orchard Street Shopping District From vintage to fashionista, discounts are door-to-door on Orchard, Grand and Delancey Streets. It's here that you get to haggle, at least a little bit. Look for leather goods, too. Lower East Side area www.lowereastsideny.com
Subway: F, J to Delancey Street–Essex Street, D to Grand Street, F to Second Avenue

17th Street Photo Hidden on the fourth floor, and a lot less hassle than the more well-known B&H, this family-run business has all the latest camera and video goodies you could want, and at the right price. 34 W 17th Street 212 366 5248 www.17photo.com
10.00–18.00 Mon–Thur, 10.00–17.30 Fri, closed Sat & Sun
Subway: F, L to 14th Street, 1 to 18th Street

TAKING A BREAK

Take a stroll through Union Square's Greenmarket, or stop in for sourdough at City Bakery on 18th Street. If you haven't seen enough museums already, visit Teddy Roosevelt's birthplace near the Park on 20th Street. People-watch from your perch at a sidewalk café in SoHo, such as Felix Bistro, or beeline it to the Lower East Side, where food is king.

Economy Candy £ ❶ Sells a huge range of candy. ⓐ 108 Rivington Street ⓣ 212 254 1531 ⓦ www.economycandy.com ⓛ 09.00–18.00 Mon–Fri & Sun, 10.00–17.00 Sat ⓝ Subway: F to Delancey Street, J, M, Z to Essex Street

Katz's Delicatessen £ ❷ Famous for its slogan, 'Send a Salami to your boy in the Army' during World War II, Katz's has been dishing out the best hand-cut pastrami and cured corned beef sandwiches since 1888 when the area was filled with Russian immigrants. ⓐ 205 E Houston Street ⓣ 212 254 2246 ⓦ www.katzdeli.com ⓛ 08.00–22.00 Sun–Tues, 08.00–23.00 Wed & Thur, 08.00–15.00 Fri & Sat ⓝ Subway: F, V to Lower East Side–Second Avenue

Kossar's £ ❸ Bialy is a bagel's cousin. ⓐ 367 Grand Street ⓣ 212 253 2146 ⓦ www.kossarsbialys.com ⓛ 06.00–20.00 Mon–Thur & Sun, 06.00–14.00 Fri ⓝ Subway: F to Delancey Street, J, M, Z to Essex Street

Russ & Daughters £ ❹ Caviar and smoked fish. ⓐ 179 E Houston Street No 1 ⓣ 212 475 4880 ⓦ www.russanddaughters.com ⓛ 09.00–19.00 Mon–Sat, 08.00–17.30 Sun ⓝ Subway: F to Second Avenue

Teany Café £ ❺ A teashop with a techno beat that has breakfast-to-late-night teany bagels. Try the tomatillo-squash soup, or any one of 98 bottled teas. ⓐ 90 Rivington Street ⓣ 212 475 9190 ⓦ www.teany.com ⓛ 10.00–23.00 Wed–Sun, 10.00–02.00 Fri & Sat ⓝ Subway: F to Delancey

Yonah Schimmel Knishery £ Delicious baked savoury snacks.
⊙ 137 E Houston Street ☏ 212 477 2858 ⓦ www.knishery.com
🕓 08.30–18.00 Ⓝ Subway: J, M to Bowery

AFTER DARK

How to choose from all the offerings is the biggest dilemma in
these areas. Be sure of one thing, though, plan for a late night.
These districts are for night owls. Trendy restaurants and bars
pop up frequently, and disappear just as fast! Besides the places
listed here, add to your dance card **APT**, or **Cielo**, and keep an eye
on who's partying over at **Avalon** (once the fabulous Limelight –
housed inside a gothic church). There are plenty of 24-hour
restaurants around, just in case you need a nibble at some
unexpected hour.

Restaurants

Inoteca £ ❼ Italian tapas, panini sandwiches and a hip wine bar.
⊙ 98 Rivington Street ☏ 212 614 0473 ⓦ www.inotecanyc.com
🕓 12.00–03.00 Mon–Fri, 10.00–03.00 Sat & Sun Ⓝ Subway: F, J, M, Z
to Delancey

Blue Smoke ££ ❽ Smoked barbecue and soulful live
jazz downstairs. ⊙ 116 E 27th Street ☏ 212 447 7733
ⓦ www.bluesmoke.com 🕓 11.30–23.00 Mon & Tues, 11.30–01.00
Wed–Fri, 12.00–01.00 Sat, 12.00–23.00 Sun Ⓝ Subway: 6 to 28th
Street

Florent ££ ❾ Low-key French bistro food you can afford in this
casual, fun place. ⊙ 69 Gansevoort Street ☏ 212 989 5779

Ⓦ www.restaurantflorent.com Ⓛ 24 hours a day Ⓝ Subway: A, C, E, to 14th Street, L to Eighth Avenue

Old Homestead ££ ⑩ This is the 'steak joint' to which New Yorkers have long journeyed, way west of 14th Street, to feast on its delicious beef, right in the heart of the old, but now disappearing, meat market. The latest mania is Kobe-burger, a pricey luxury. Ⓐ 56 Ninth Avenue Ⓣ 212 807 0707 Ⓦ www.oldhomesteadsteakhouse.com Ⓛ 12.00–22.45 Mon–Fri, 12.00–23.45 Sat, 01.00–21.45 Sun Ⓝ Subway: A, C, E to 14th Street–Eighth Avenue, L, 1, 2, 3, to 14th Street

Upstairs at Bouley ££ ⑪ Try the new Bouley Burger in Chef David's second-line place. Ⓐ 130 W Broadway Ⓣ 212 219 1011 Ⓦ www.davidbouley.com Ⓛ 17.00–24.00 Mon–Sat, closed Sun Ⓝ Subway: 1, 2, 3 to Chambers Street

Chanterelle £££ ⑫ Dine at the late night, long-standing Tribeca pick of other restaurateurs. Relax in Queen Anne chairs while dining

🔺 *Funky paints adorn this doorway*

under the soft light of chandeliers. Try their tasting menu.
2 Harrison Street 212 966 6960 www.chanterellenyc.com
12.00–14.30 Thur–Sat, 17.30–22.30 Mon–Fri 17.30–23.00 Sat, closed
Sun Subway: A, C, 1, 2, 3 to Chambers Street

Union Square Café £££ Long popular with locals who come
for Michael Romano's dinner specials, and the murals. 21 E 16th
Street 212 243 4020 www.unionsquarecafe.com 12.00–14.45
Mon–Sun, 17.30–21.45 Sun–Thur, 17.30–10.45 Fri & Sat Subway: L, N,
R, Q, W, 6 to 14th Street–Union Square

Cinemas & theatres

Angelika Film Center's place for artsy independent films. 18 W
Houston Street 212 995 2000 www.angelikafilmcenter.com
Films start 10.45–24.00 Mon–Sun Subway: B, D, F, Q to
Broadway–Lafayette Street, N, R, to Prince Street

Bars, clubs & discos

BED NY Plush pillows, nibbles and drinks, all on a bed. 530 W 27th
Street 212 594 4109 www.bedny.com 19.00–24.00 Tues–Thur,
19.00–01.00 Fri & Sat; Bar until 04.00 Tues–Sat, 24.00 Sun
Subway: C, E to 23rd Street

Bowery Ballroom A standing rock music venue in an old beaux arts
building with state-of-the art sound. Show tickets required.
6 Delancey Street 212 533 2111 www.boweryballroom.com
19.00–04.00 Mon–Sun Subway: F to Second Avenue, B, D to
Grand Street, J, M to Bowery, 6 to Spring Street

The skyline overlooking Gramercy Park

Brooklyn

'Don't buy the Brooklyn Bridge!' is an often-heard, age-old warning not to be gullible. Several swindlers actually sold the bridge after it was built, and ended up in Sing Sing Jail. Brooklyn Bridge was America's first steel suspension bridge, and thousands walk across its 1,834 m (6,016 ft) long footbridge every day. The views across to Manhattan are nothing less than spectacular, day and night. You can get to Brooklyn in less than ten minutes on a subway, but to enjoy the vistas, opt to walk over; go by water taxi (ⓦ www.nywatertaxi.com), or take the hop-on-and-off tour bus (ⓦ www.newyorksightseeing.com), which stops at several of Brooklyn's main attractions.

Brooklyn is big enough both in area and population to be America's third largest city. It has enough attractions to fill an entire holiday – everything from beluga caviar to beluga whales. Its original name, Breuckelen, comes from its Dutch settlers. The borough is filled with ethnic diversity: Latinos from the Caribbean settled in Flatbush, and Polish groups made Greenpoint their home. Italians and Chinese live predominantly in the Sunset Park area. Williamsburg has enclaves of Hispanics, and Hasidic Jews, and just to the southeast is the largely African-American Bedford Stuyvesant neighbourhood. There are so many Russians in Brighton Beach and Coney Island, that it is known as Little Odessa.

SIGHTS & ATTRACTIONS

Brooklynites live in a small town atmosphere with a tempered pace. Early residents built many beautiful homes and stately mansions, happily unscathed by the march of skyscrapers. Near the waterfront

Brooklyn

0   500 metres

0   500 yards

in Brooklyn Heights, the city's first designated historic district, you can walk along the sleepy streets and see Greek Revival and Italianate row houses. The Brooklyn Heights Promenade is a great place to picnic while taking in fabulous views. Its close neighbour, Boreum, also has beautiful homes, as does Park Slope with its old Victorian brownstones.

Nearby is **Prospect Park**, which rivals Manhattan's Central Park (made by the same designers). Its lush rolling landscape, with waterfalls and reflecting pools, offers visitors a carousel, an ice rink, the zoo, and free summer concerts at the Bandshell. Grand Army Plaza, with its towering Arch, marks the entrance to the Park and the **Brooklyn Botanic Garden** (Ⓦ www.bbg.org), famous for its Cherry blossom Esplanade.

CULTURE

Of the many cultural venues, BAM or **Brooklyn Academy of Music** (Ⓦ www.bam.org) boasts its own symphony orchestra, and the innovative Next Wave Festival. Also here are the Rose Cinemas, and on weekend nights BAM Café comes alive with country and hip-hop. **The Brooklyn Museum** (Ⓦ www.brooklynmuseum.org) has 1.5 million objects, including a renowned Egyptology collection, and wonderful paintings by Edgar Degas, Georgia O'Keefe and others. Emerging artists have taken over the cobblestoned streets Down Under the Manhattan Bridge Overpass, known simply as DUMBO, and the gentrified area now has many boutiques, restaurants and art galleries and events.

❿ *Cross the Brooklyn Bridge for the best views of Manhattan*

TAKING A BREAK

Get away from urban blight in a bird look-out post at the Jamaica
Bay Wildlife Refuge (ⓦ www.nps.gov/gate). Swim at nearby
Coney Island Beach in summer, or test your vocal chords while
screaming on the Cyclone roller coaster at Astroland Amusement
Park (ⓦ www.astroland.com). Visit New York's only Aquarium
(ⓦ www.nyaquarium.com), but it's not cool to be seen with a
Nathan's Famous hot dog in one hand, and caviar in the other.
There's hardly time for shopping, but stop by Atlantic Avenue for
antiques, or try Aaron's (ⓦ www.aarons.com) for designer bargains.
Boutiques are now popping up in all the neighbourhoods.

Brooklyn Ice Cream Factory £ ❶ Put on calories with a double
scoop here. ⓐ 2 Old Fulton Street, Brooklyn ❶ 718 246 3963

Junior's ££ ❷ Try their famous cheesecake. ⓐ 386 Flatbush Avenue
Ext., Brooklyn ❶ 718 852 5257

AFTER DARK

If daytime Brooklyn's your scene, then you'll love immersing yourself
in this atmospheric area's plethora of places to eat, drink and be
seen after hours.

◀ *Distinctive Brooklyn diner on 57th Street*

Restaurants

Al Di Là Trattoria £–££ ❸ There's a queue out the door for the risotto in this funky, packed place. ⓐ 248 Fifth Avenue, Brooklyn ⓣ 718 636 8888

Alma ££ ❹ Mexican fare on the rooftop deck. ⓐ 187 Columbia Street, Brooklyn ⓣ 718 643 5400

Blue Ribbon ££–£££ ❺ Known for its multi-ethnic menu and it's kid-friendly, too. ⓐ 280 Fifth Avenue, Brooklyn ⓣ 718 840 0404

Applewood £££ ❻ Slow food, wholesome meats and wild fish. ⓐ 501 11th Street, Brooklyn ⓣ 718 768 2044

Peter Luger's £££ ❼ Prime beef and sizzling steaks that melt in your mouth. ⓐ 178 Broadway, Brooklyn ⓣ 718 387 7400

River Café £££ ❽ Exudes romance and a fabulous view from the waterfront. ⓐ 1 Water Street, Brooklyn ⓣ 718 522 5200

ⓘ Watch for Restaurant Week special rates at some of these restaurants.

ⓓ *Choose your pickles carefully*

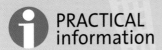

Directory

GETTING THERE

New York is conveniently located at the centre of the Northeast Corridor, the name used for several major East Coast cities, including major transit hubs – Boston, Baltimore and Washington, DC. The New York metropolitan area is serviced by both JFK and Newark airports. These Northeast Corridor cities are close enough that you can travel from them to New York by air, rail, bus and car.

By air

Large international airlines provide morning direct flight services to New York and the Northeast Corridor from the UK. British Airways (ⓦ www.britishairways.com), Virgin Atlantic Airways (ⓦ www.virgin.com/uk), and American Airlines (ⓦ www.aa.com) fly from Heathrow with a dozen or so flights each day to JFK and Newark. Continental Airlines (ⓦ www.continental.com) has several daily flights from Gatwick to Newark. British Airways, Virgin and American Airlines also fly to Boston. BA goes to both Baltimore-Washington International (BWI) and Washington (Dulles). United (ⓦ www.united.com) and Virgin also fly to Washington (Dulles). Fares are pretty competitive on all these airlines, so you may choose the one you feel comfortable with. You can fly from Stansted on Maxjet (ⓦ www.maxjet.com) or EOS (ⓦ www.eosairlines.com) to New York (JFK).

If you want to travel from Boston or Washington to New York by air, consider the frequent domestic flights that go into Laguardia airport, which is closer to the city and a cheaper taxi ride. US

▶ *Flying the stars and stripes*

Airways (ⓦ www.usairways.com) has a Shuttle service every hour from Boston (🕐 06.00–20.00), and from Washington, DC (🕐 07.00–21.00, slightly reduced service on weekends). The Washington Shuttle leaves from Reagan National, close to the city's centre.

Many people are aware that air travel emits CO_2, which contributes to climate change. You may be interested in the possibility of lessening the environmental impact of your flight through the charity Climate Care, which offsets your CO_2 by funding environmental projects around the world. Visit www.climatecare.org

By train

Travelling to New York by train is a pleasure. Amtrak's (ⓦ www.amtrak.com) Aceia Express leaves Union Station in Washington, DC and arrives at New York Penn Station 2 hours 50 minutes later. Amtrak has a station right at BWI, so if you're leaving from that area, it might be wise to fly into BWI in the first place; getting to Union Station from Dulles is a little more complicated.

From Boston's South Station, it's a 3 hour 30 minute train ride (on the same Aceia Express), and you'll see all the New England states on your way to New York. The most obvious advantages of going by train are that it's usually punctual, it takes far less time than buses and cars, which can get delayed in traffic and tunnels. The brand new Silver Line (ⓦ www.allaboutsilverline.com) rapid transit direct service operates between Boston's South Station and Logan airport.

By bus

LimoLiner (ⓦ www.limoliner.com) is a new and innovative bus service from Boston to New York. This company wants its passengers to travel in a civilised fashion – leather bucket seats (only aisle or window), free fruit and cheese to munch on while surfing the net from a seat-side socket, and mobile phone reception – all this and four hours gets you to New York. Washington Deluxe (ⓦ www.washny.com) also has premium service to New York, but without so many perks. Tried and trusted is Greyhound (ⓦ www.greyhound.com), which can get you to New York's Port Authority Terminal from just about anywhere in the US. The service to New York from Boston and Washington is about once every hour.

By road

Car rental places are plentiful, just be sure to reserve ahead. Some savings can be had with a fly-drive package, but leave those four wheels far behind when you arrive in Manhattan. Avoid rush hours and late-Sunday afternoon in summer.

ⓘ It's illegal to drive with a mobile phone in your hand.

ENTRY FORMALITIES

Visa requirements

Most citizens of the UK, Ireland, Canada, New Zealand, Australia and Singapore with a valid machine readable passport don't need a visa to visit the US for pleasure, on certain types of business, or in transit, if their stay will be for fewer than 90 days; this is part of the Visa Waiver Programme. All passports issued after this date must include biometric data and a digital photograph. Children must have their own separate machine-readable passports. Travellers must hold a return or onward ticket. If travelling on an electronic ticket, you will need a copy of the itinerary. You must also complete form I-94W, which is available from airline companies. This form will require the address where you will be staying, including the zip code. All citizens will need a visa if they have been arrested, have a criminal record, or have a serious disease, including HIV. Citizens of Israel and South Africa must have visas to enter the US. It is advisable that the passport be renewed if it is valid for less than six months. For more information contact the US Embassy (ⓦ www.usembassy.org.uk).

Customs

Adults visiting the US are allowed one carton of cigarettes or 50 cigars, and a litre of liquor. They may also carry with them $100/£53 worth of gifts, free of duty. Currency or monetary instruments worth over $10,000/£5,300 are permitted but must be reported (coming in or going out). Customs forms to fill out are provided on inbound flights, so have your passport number handy.

Prescription medicine is permitted, but those containing narcotics require a statement or prescription from their doctor for those particular drugs, and all medicines should be in clearly marked containers. Most foods, fruits, meats and plants are off limits, with few exceptions, so leave them behind. If you want to dig deeper into all the regulations, go to the US Customs website (ⓦ www.customs.gov). On the way home, you'll have to comply with UK allowances, which are rather limited.

MONEY

The US dollar ($) is the basic unit of currency, divided into 100 cents. Dollar bills (paper money called 'greenbacks') come in denominations of $1, $2, $5, $10, $20, $50 and $100. The $2 bill is rarely seen, as they are traditionally kept as souvenirs. Even though these days the single dollar will hardly buy anything, coins adding up to 100 cents, which equal $1, are in regular use. There's a copper penny (1¢), silver-colour nickels (5¢), dimes (10¢), quarters (25¢), half-dollars (50¢), and a dollar coin, which is really easy to mistake for a quarter. Fortunately, the half-dollar and dollar coins are rarely seen. While the US treasury has remodelled various bills, they're still all the same size, so don't give away $100, when only $1 is due! Don't carry large amounts of cash, but if you're out clubbing for the night, cash may be the only option. Some shopkeepers and cashiers are wary about breaking the larger $50 and $100 bills, and cabbies don't have to change anything over $5, so do that at your hotel or a bank. Currency exchange and ATMs are easily found in airports, transit stations, at banks and even in supermarkets.

Be sure not to leave home without enough money for unexpected extras. Dollar traveller's cheques are more convenient; buy them in smaller amounts up to $100/£53. Bring more than one credit card (check card limits before you leave), and some cash for a coffee or an urgency during the trip. New York has quite a few restaurants and cafés that don't accept credit cards. Put credit card and traveller's cheque numbers somewhere safe, and while you travel don't keep everything in one place. Visa, MasterCard, American Express and Diners Club are the most recognised cards. Banks in New York are open 09.00–15.00 Mon–Fri, and sometimes later.

Prices are stated exclusive of sales tax! Expect to pay 8.375 per cent tax on almost everything, including restaurant and hotel bills, but not food bought in a grocery store, or clothes and shoe purchases under $110/£58. Sales tax on goods purchased is administered by the state, and no refunds are possible. Hotel rates have an additional tax as well.

HEALTH, SAFETY & CRIME

In any big city, especially one you don't know, it's better to be safe than sorry. That means being aware of what's going on around you. Keep cameras and handbags secure; they'll disappear without a trace if you lay them down while shopping. The ever-lowering crime rate is thanks to the vigilance of New York's recent mayors. It also has a lot to do with gentrification in every nook and cranny of Manhattan. Places like the East Village, the Lower East Side, Alphabet City, Hell's Kitchen, Harlem, and even Bed-Stuy (Bedford-Stuyvesant in Brooklyn), that once were termed 'Avoid at all cost!', are being rejuvenated with condos, boutiques and cafés. Don't be 'midtown mugger bait' with map in hand, neck strained upward, gawping at a skyscraper. New York police make safety a priority. They wear dark blue uniforms and can be very helpful. Treat them with respect. For what to do in an emergency, see page 154. Since 9/11, security checks are common in large buildings, and now bags and luggage are checked in subway stations, so always carry a picture ID (preferably not your passport). For any incident involving the police, such as a theft, ask for a report.

New York water is clean, and most people drink water from the tap. Take bottled water in your bag for refreshment on the run.

Unless you wish to come into close contact with a vehicle's bumper, remember that you're probably looking *left*, when you should be looking *right*, so be sure to look *both* ways before stepping off the curb. Otherwise, you could be part of a medical emergency. Medical treatment in hospitals is prohibitively expensive in the US, and it is essential that you carry comprehensive travel and medical insurance. At least $1,000,000 cover is recommended, to include hospital treatment and medical evacuation to the UK. Check the small print and exclusions, especially if you engage in sports.

Carry prescription medicines and spectacles in your hand luggage, and take extra prescription specs, in case one pair is broken or lost. In case of a life-threatening emergency you can dial 911 from any telephone for free. See Emergencies, page 154.

Bring appropriate clothing for the season. Layers are best for winter (average −3 to 3°C), with a warm coat, and very light clothes for summer (average 20 to 29°C). If the weather man is saying its 32° out there, that means 0°C to you.

LOCAL LAWS

You must be age 21 to buy or be served alcohol in New York, and you must be 18 to buy tobacco products. Restaurant and bar servers may ask for anyone's photo ID to verify age. If you drive, there is *no right turn on red* anywhere in New York City. Look for signs indicating special turn rules. You can be fined $50/£27 if your mobile rings (and you are caught and cited) during theatre, concerts, movies or the ballet, so remember to turn it off before the performance starts. The same rule applies in a public library.

OPENING HOURS

In the city that never sleeps it's difficult to pin down when things are open and when they are closed, but generally speaking the place is open 9 to 5 (🕐 09.00 to 17.00), at least in the worker's world on weekdays. Banks are open at least 09.00–15.00 weekdays. Shops open at 09.00 or 10.00 and close at 18.00 or later. Pharmacies and supermarkets are usually open by 08.00 and stay open late; some never close. Most Duane Reade pharmacies are open 24 hours a day. Major attractions and museums open by 09.00 or 10.00, and while many museums are closed at least one day of the week, they usually keep evening hours on one day.

TOILETS

New York's biggest mystery – what to do when you've got to go!
There's actually a website to help solve this problem
(ⓦ www.nyrestroom.com). Luckily, there are lots of solutions – most
of the public libraries, bookstores, museums and large department
stores have clean toilets. You can go in with the animals at the Central
Park Zoo (in the public toilet, of course), and there are various other
facilities in the Park. Bars, and hotels with large lobbies, are good
options, too. A quick stop at any fast-food store should provide relief.

🔺 *Fresh produce in Chinatown*

CHILDREN

Make sure your child has their own passport. Hotels usually provide cots for babies, at no additional charge. Supermarkets have whole aisles devoted to baby and children products, such as nappies. Plenty of neighbourhood eateries are glad to serve the whole family, or try some of the many theme restaurants. Alternatively, just get a pizza – New York crusts are unsurpassed.

Activities run the gamut:

- **Children's Museum of Manhattan** Whiz down Boot's Treehouse. Ⓦ www.cmom.org
- **Circle Line** Cruises on the River Hudson. Ⓦ www.circleline.com
- **Coney Island** Ride the CYCLONE! Ⓦ www.astroland.com
- **Intrepid Sea-Air-Space Museum** An aircraft carrier, aircraft on deck, and the Navy Flight Simulator. Ⓦ www.intrepidmuseum.org
- **Lazer Tag** Ⓦ www.lazerpark.com
- **Sony Wonder Tech Lab** Four floors of hands-on-electronic-everything. Make a reservation. Ⓦ www.sonywondertechlab.com
- **Toys " Я" Us** Ride the *indoor* Ferris wheel. Ⓦ www4.toysrus.com
- **Trapeze School** Trot your teens off for some high flying. Ⓦ www.newyork.trapezeschool.com
- **WildLife Habitat** Watch seal feeding time at the zoo. Ⓦ www.nyzoosandaquarium.com

COMMUNICATIONS
Phones

When making a long-distance telephone call, it is necessary to dial the number 1 before dialling the area code and number. In New York, you must dial 1 plus the area code even for local calls. If you call the

British Consulate in Manhattan, you dial (1) 212 745 0200. Telephone codes for Manhattan are 212 and 646, and in the boroughs, 718 and 347. The code 917 is for cell phones. Codes 800, 866, 877 and 888 are toll-free. A good general rule is never to dial out from a hotel room; you can find a public telephone in the hotel lobby, and dialling 800 numbers doesn't require a coin. To make international calls, dial 011, + country code + number.

Internet

New York is wired. There's wi-fi all over, from hostels to hotels, in public libraries, in cafés, and even in Bryant Park. The latest item to hit the streets is plug-in access at pay phones (you can connect to Ⓦ www.nycvisit.com free of charge). The easyInternetcafé in

Telephone New York from the UK: dial 001 + city code + number
Telephone the US from the UK: dial 001 + city code + number
Telephone the UK from New York: dial 011 + 44 + number
Telephone Canada from New York: dial 011 + 1 + city code + number
Telephone Australia from New York: dial 011 + 61 + city code + number

New York has important, easy, 24-hour, special use numbers:
911 is for emergencies such as a serious accident.
311 is New York City's call centre phone number for government information and non-emergency services.
411 is used to obtain local Manhattan telephone numbers, usually a free call when made from a public telephone.

Times Square is the world's largest, with over 600 PCs (🅐 234 W 42nd Street 🕐 07.00–01.00 🅦 www.easyinternetcafe.com).

Post

Stamps can be obtained at local post offices, from drugstore vending machines, and at newsstands. Dark blue post boxes are located on some street corners, with a rounded top, and information about collection times. Express Mail arrives anywhere in the US by the next day, and takes about two to three days to the UK, but it needs a form and a trip to the post office. The main post office at 421 Eighth Avenue is open 24 hours a day (🅦 www.usps.com).

ELECTRICITY

Throughout the United States, electric current is 110–120V, 60Hz AC. You can buy adaptors at the airport, in department stores, and in hardware stores. US plugs are flat-pin.

TRAVELLERS WITH DISABILITIES

Under both New York and federal law, facilities built after 1987 must provide access for people with disabilities. However, the city can still be difficult to negotiate for anyone with a disability. The Mayor's Office for People with Disabilities (🅣 212 788 2830) will send the book *Access New York* free of charge upon request by telephone. It has specific accessibility information for theatres, sports venues, and more. The city's buses are equipped with lifts for wheelchair users – the going might be slow, but you can get anywhere in the city. Some, but not all, subway stations have lifts or ramps. The Hands On! Organization arranges sign language interpreting for many New York cultural events. All the major museums are accessible, as well as many of the galleries. Most hotels have specially fitted rooms for people with disabilities, and restaurants in hotels and their toilet facilities are properly equipped. Difficult places to get around could be the tiny streets of Chinatown, and the little subterranean restaurants.

FURTHER INFORMATION
Tourist offices
New York City's Official Visitor Information Center ⓐ 810 Seventh Avenue ① 212 484 1222 ⓒ 08.30–18.00 Mon–Fri, 08.30–17.00 Sat & Sun ⓦ www.nycvisit.com

Information points
Brooklyn Tourism and Visitors Center ⓐ Borough Hall, 209 Joralem Street ⓒ 10.00–18.00 Mon–Fri

Harlem Visitor Information Kiosk ⓐ 163 W 125th Street ⓒ 09.00–18.00 Mon–Fri, 10.00–06.00 Sat & Sun

NYC Heritage Tourism Center City Hall Park ⓐ Park Row ⓒ 09.00–18.00 Mon–Fri, 10.00–18.00 Sat & Sun

Official Visitor Information Kiosk for Chinatown ⓐ Junction of Canal and Walker ⓒ 10.00–18.00 Sun–Fri, 10.00–19.00 Sat

Many neighbourhoods have formed alliances, and their websites give local information. A few are listed here:

Alliance for Downtown New York ⓦ www.downtownny.com
The Bronx Tourism Council ⓦ www.ilovethebronx.com

The Lesbian, Gay, Bisexual & Transgender Community Center
Ⓦ www.gaycenter.org

Lincoln Square Business Improvement District
Ⓦ www.lincolnbid.org

Madison Avenue Business Improvement District
Ⓦ www.madisonavenuebid.org

SoHoNYC.com Ⓦ www.sohonyc.com

Times Square Alliance Ⓦ www.timessquarenyc.org

Tribeca Organization Ⓦ www.tribeca.org

BACKGROUND READING

O'Henry spent many years living in Greenwich Village; his sensitive stories about the human soul and heart are set against the fabric of New York – *The Gift of the Magii*. Set in modern times, Tom Wolfe must have pounded the sidewalks of the Upper East Side to give us *Bonfire of Vanities*. Another true New York setting by J D Salinger is found in *Catcher in the Rye*. A E Hotchner shares the scoop on an iconic New York hostess in *Everyone Comes to Elaine's*.

Emergencies

POLICE

In case of a life-threatening emergency, you can dial **911** from any telephone for free. The number 911 is reserved for extremely urgent needs. State your name, location, and the nature of the problem. You can also dial 0 to get operator assistance. If you need to contact the police for any other reason, such as theft, call 636 610 5000 for police information and to locate the nearest police precinct. If you make a report to the police, make sure you request a copy. If the nature of the problem is serious, be sure to let them know that you are a foreigner visiting the US, and request to speak with a consular officer of your home country.

MEDICAL

If your emergency is serious, dial **911** and, if necessary, request an ambulance. If an ambulance is not necessary, take a taxi to the nearest hospital. If your emergency is not serious, you have several options to receive medical service. Before you leave home, you can make a short list of physicians, clinics and hospitals, which is available through the International Association for Medical Assistance to Travellers (IAMAT – ⓦ www.iamat.org). The association is free to join (they suggest a donation), and has a comprehensive directory of medical services and required immunisations. IAMAT's English-speaking doctors have reasonable set fees. For minor ailments, you can go to a clinic, which requires payment upon service, but this should be less costly than a hospital emergency room. DOCS Physicians has a walk-in clinic for a reasonable fee

---

▶ *It may be pretty, but snow can cause hazardous conditions*

for primary care, but try to go early to avoid long waiting times. TravelMD.com has a 24-hours Urgent Care Center, and sees patients by appointment. It also provides in-hotel medical service through its physicians and dentists network. Hospitals are located in nearly every neighbourhood.

Cabrini Medical Center ⓐ 227 E 19th Street ⓣ 212 995 6000
DOCS Physicians Walk-In Clinic ⓐ 55 E 34th Street ⓣ 212 252 6000
ⓒ 08.00–20.00 Mon–Thur, until 19.00 Fri, 09.00–15.00 Sat, 09.00–14.00 Sun
Mount Sinai Hospital ⓐ 100th Street and Madison Avenue
ⓣ 212 241 7171
St Luke's-Roosevelt Hospital ⓐ 1000 Tenth Avenue ⓣ 212 523 6800
St Vincent's Hospital ⓐ 153 W 11th Street ⓣ 212 604 7998
TravelMD.com ⓐ Urgent Care Center or NY Hotel Urgent Medical Services ⓐ 952 Fifth Avenue ⓣ 212 737 1212 ⓒ 24 hours a day
ⓦ www.travelmd.com

Police/Fire/Ambulance ⓣ 911
Medical Emergencies ⓣ 800 395 3400
Crime Victims Hotline ⓣ 212 577 7777
NYC Subway and Bus Information ⓣ 718 330 1234 ⓦ www.mta.info
Taxi & Limousine Commission ⓣ 212 302 8294 ⓦ www.nyc.gov/taxi
Towed Cars ⓣ 212 869 2929
Main Post Office ⓣ 212 967 8585

EMBASSIES & CONSULATES

Australian Consulate ⓦ www.australianyc.org ☎ 212 351 6500

British Consulate General ⓐ 845 Third Avenue, New York, NY
☎ 212 745 0200 🖶 212 745 3062 ⓦ www.britainusa.com/ny

Canadian Consulate ☎ 212 596 1628 ⓦ www.dfait-maeci.gc.ca/new_york

New Zealand Consulate ☎ 212 832 4038

Republic of Ireland ☎ 212 319 2555 ⓔ congenny@aol.com

South Africa ☎ 212 213 4880 ⓦ www.southafrica-newyork.net

INDEX

The publishers would like to thank the following for supplying the copyright photographs for this book: BED New York: page 17; Gershwin Hotel: page 34; Jerry Grymek: page 48; Pictures Colour Library: pages 1, 7, 13, 21, 27, 28, 45, 48, 61, 70, 89, 96–97; Robert McCabe: page 155; Randa Bishop: all other photographs.

Copy editor: Joanne Osborn
Proofreader: Jenni Rainford-Hairsine

Send your thoughts to
books@thomascook.com

- Found a great bar, club, shop or must-see sight that we don't feature?

- Like to tip us off about any information that needs updating?

- Want to tell us what you love about this handy little guidebook and, more importantly, how we can make it even handier?

Then here's your chance to tell all! Send us ideas, discoveries and recommendations today and then look out for your valuable input in the next edition of this title. As an extra 'thank you' from Thomas Cook Publishing, you'll be automatically entered into our exciting monthly prize draw.

Send an email to the above address (stating the book's title) or write to: CitySpots Project Editor, Thomas Cook Publishing, PO Box 227, The Thomas Cook Business Park, Unit 18, Coningsby Road, Peterborough PE3 8SB, UK.